Sacr

By Nigel Pennick

Sacred Geometry

©1994 Nigel Pennick

ISBN 1 898307 15 6

ALL RIGHTS RESERVED

No part of this publication may be reproduced, stored in a retrieval system or transmitted in any form or by any means, electronic, mechanical, photocopying, scanning, recording or otherwise without the prior written permission of the author and the publisher.

Cover illustration by Nigel Pennick
Cover design by Daryth Bastin

Published by:

Capall Bann Publishing
Freshfields
Chieveley
Berks
RG16 8TF

Contents

Introduction	1
1. The Principles of Sacred Geometry	5
2. The Forms	15
3. Ancient British Geometry	30
4. Ancient Egyptian Sacred Geometry	47
5. Mesopotamian and Hebrew Sacred Geometry	62
6. Ancient Greece	74
7. Vitruvius	83
8. The Comacines and Medieval Sacred Geometry	91
9. Masonic Symbolism and Documentary Evidence	107
10. Problems, Conflicts and Divulgence of the Mysteries	120
11. Renaissance Sacred Geometry	131
12. Baroque Geometry	147
13. Sacred Geometry in Exile	157
14. Science: The Verifier of Sacred Geometry	175
Index	183

To Albertus Argentinus, inventor of
ad quadratum.

Each molecule throughout the universe bears impressed upon it the stamp of a metric system, as distinctly as does the metre of the archives of Paris, or the double Royal Cubit of the Temple at Karnak.

Sir William Herschel

Sacred Geometry

In this absorbing history, the first of its kind, the applications of sacred geometry in religious architecture are examined and the full extent of its practice, from stone circles and medieval cathedrals to Baroque churches and Art Nouveau, is revealed.

Sacred Geometry

Introduction

Man is the measure of all things, of being things that they exist, and of nonentities that they do not exist.

> Protagoras (c.481-411 B.C.)

Geometry exists everywhere in nature: its order underlies the structure of all things from molecules to galaxies, from the smallest virus to the largest whale. Despite our separation from the natural world, we human beings are still bounded by the natural laws of the universe. The unique consciously-planned artifacts of mankind have, since the earliest times, likewise been based upon systems of geometry. These systems, although initially derived from natural forms, often exceeded them in complexity and ingenuity, and were imbued with magic powers and profound psychological meaning.

Geometry, literally 'the measuring of the earth', was perhaps one of the earliest manifestations of nascent civilization. The fundamental tool which underlies all that is made by the hands of people, geometry developed out of an even earlier skill - the handling of measure, which in ancient times was considered to be a branch of magic. At that early period, magic, science and religion were in fact inseparable, being part of the corpus of skills possessed by the priesthood.

Sacred Geometry

The earliest religions of humanity were focused upon those natural places at which the numinous quality of the earth could be readily felt: among trees, rocks, springs, in caves and high places. The function of the priesthood that grew up around such sites of natural sanctity was at first interpretative. Priests and priestesses were the specialists who could read meaning into auguries and oracles, storms, winds, earthquakes and other manifestations of the universe's energies.

The arts of shamanism that the earliest priests practised gave way with increasing sophistication to a settled ritual priesthood that required outward symbols of the faith. No longer were unhewn boulders and isolated trees the sole requirement of a place of worship. Enclosures were laid out, demarcated as special holy places separate from the profane world. In the ritual required by this laying-out, geometry became inseparably connected with religious activity.

The harmony inherent in geometry was early recognised as the most cogent expression of a divine plan which underlies the world, a metaphysical pattern which determines the physical. This inner reality, transcendent of outer form, has remained throughout history the basis of sacred structures. Hence, it is just as valid today to construct a modern building according to the principles of sacred geometry as it was in the past in such styles as Egyptian, Classical, Romanesque, Islamic, Gothic, Renaissance or Art Nouveau. Proportion and harmony naturally follow the exercise of sacred geometry, which looks right because it is right, being linked metaphysically with the esoteric structure of matter.

Sacred geometry is inextricably linked with various mystical tenets. Perhaps the most important of these is that attributed to the alchemists' founder Hermes Trismegistus, the Thrice Great Hermes. This maxim is the fundamental 'As above, so below', or 'That which is in the lesser world (the microcosm) reflects that of the greater world or universe (the macrocosm)'. This theory of correspondences underlies all of astrology and much alchemy, geomancy and magic, where the form of the universal creation is reflected in the body and constitution of man.

Man in turn is seen in the Hebraic conception of having been created in the image of God - the temple ordained by the Creator to house the spirit which raises man above the animal kingdom. Thus, sacred geometry treats not only of the proportions of the geometrical figures obtained in the classical manner by straightedge and compasses, but of the harmonic relations of the parts of the human being with one another; the structure of plants and animals; the forms of crystals and natural objects, all of which are manifestations of the universal continuum.

Sacred Geometry

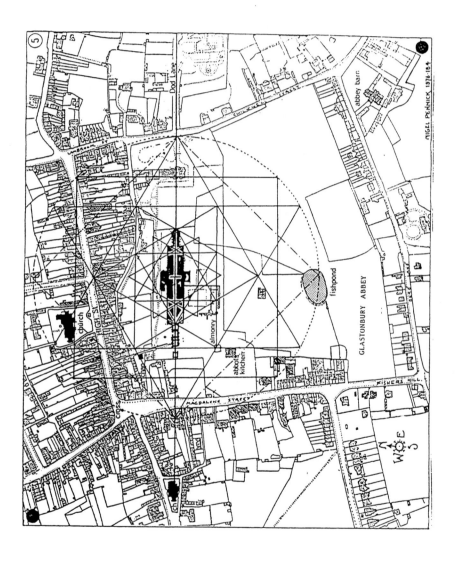

1. The Principles of Sacred Geometry

The principles that underlie disciplines such as geomancy, sacred geometry, magic or electronics are fundamentally linked with the nature of the universe. Variations in external form may be dictated by the varying tenets of different religions or even political groupings, but the operative fundamentals remain constant. An analogy with electricity may be made. In order to illuminate an electric light bulb, various conditions must be fulfilled. A certain current must be fed to the bulb by means of insulated conductors with a complete circuit, etc. These conditions are not negotiable. If something is done incorrectly, the bulb will not light. Technicians throughout the world must adhere to the fundamental principles or otherwise fail. The principles transcend political or sectarian considerations. If done properly, the circuit will function equally well in a communist state, under a military dictatorship or in a democratic country - even on another planet.

Similarly, with sacred geometry, the underlying principles transcend sectarian religious considerations. As a technology which aims to reintegrate humanity with the cosmic whole, it will work, like electricity, for anyone who fulfils the criteria, no matter what their principles or aims. The universal application of the identical principles of sacred geometry in places separated by vast gulfs of time, place and belief attests to its transcendental nature. Thus, sacred geometry has been applied to pagan temples of the Sun, shrines of Isis, tabernacles of Jehovah, sanctuaries of Marduk, martyria of Christian saints, Islamic mosques and mausolea of kings and holy ones. In every case, the thread of immutable principles connects these sacred structures.

Geometry is normally included in the discipline of mathematics; however, numerical mathematics is in fact derived from geometry, which is of a much more fundamental order than the manipulation of numbers, which is the creation of man.

Nowadays, geometrical ratios are invariably expressed in mathematical terms and it seems unthinkable that geometry could be separated from mathematics. However, the mathematical expression of ratios like pi and the golden section are merely conveniences geared to a literate civilization schooled in figures and calculation. Being primarily concerned with ratios and relationships, geometry's expression in terms of number belongs to a late period in its development. The complex geometry of ancient Egypt, which enabled architects and geometers to measure the exact size of the country, set down geodetic markers, and erect vast structures like the pyramids, was a practical art whose relationship with number was implicit. The Greek geometers, whose knowledge they admitted came from the Egyptians, likewise remained at the practical level and did not venture into the realms of complex mathematics which exist only to prove that which is already known. In fact, it was not until the seventeenth century with the rise of the peculiarly Protestant European cult of science that the precise calculation of irrational numbers became a pressing concern.

The Principles of Sacred Geometry

The interpretation of geometry in terms of numerical relationships is a later intellectual rationalisation of a natural system for the division of space. Such an interpretation came with the divorce of geometry from that corpus of science, magic and metaphysics which now goes by the name of ancient religion. Many ratios in length, for example the square roots of most whole numbers, cannot be expressed in terms of whole numbers, and thus can only be properly described in geometrical terms. Similarly the division of the circle into 360 units known as degrees in the conventional Babylonian system is not absolute. Although it is geometrically derived, it is merely a matter of convenience.

However, number, as expressed in the sacred dimensions of holy buildings, has often been used to camouflage their underlying sacred geometry. The Hebrew Tabernacle and Temple described in the Bible, and the dimensions of King's College Chapel in Cambridge, are laid down as measurements which may be interpreted by the cognoscenti in terms of mystical geometry. King Henry VI could only lay down the form of his Chapel at Cambridge in terms of measures lest he divulged the masonic mysteries to the uninitiated. Reginald Ely, his master mason, had then only to draw out the dimensions as a plan to determine the ad triangulum geometry inherent in those dimensions. *

Because geometry is an image of the structure of the cosmos, it can readily be used as a symbolic system for understanding various features of the universe. This symbolic function is exemplified by a little-known scientific instrument which was used in pre- colonial times to teach Polynesian boys the fundamentals of navigation. Although the Polynesians did not have any of the instruments now considered necessary for navigation, the sextant, compass and chronometer, they were

*See my Mysteries of King's College Chapel (Thorsons 1978)

Sacred Geometry

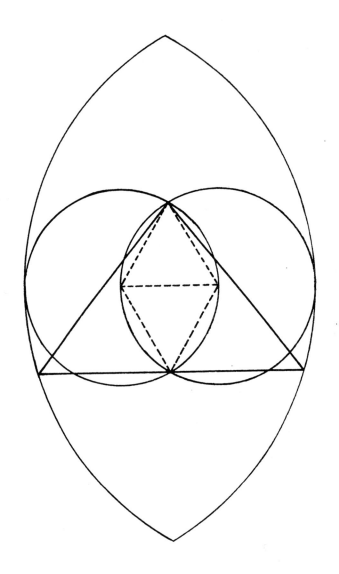

1. The Vesica Piscis with the outline of the Great Pyramid.

able to travel regularly across great expanses of ocean and reach their objectives. Using the stars and other physical features like the presence of cloud banks over land, Polynesian navigators could detect the presence of islands, but the most useful method was by reading the waves. Just as any object in the sea, like a rock, will have an effect on the pattern of the ripples, so on a much larger scale will the presence of an island cause diffraction patterns in the waves many miles away.

The science of wave recognition was taught to the boys by means of a mnemonic system, the mattang. In its form, this instrument, composed of sticks arranged in a precise geometrical pattern, was uncannily like European sacred geometry. This geometrical device demonstrated to the pupils all of the basic patterns which waves form when deflected by land. Likewise, all geometrical patterns reflect further truths far beyond their simple derivations, even the complex relationships with other geometries. Their structure is at one with the universe and all the physical, structural and psychological forces which make up its oneness.

Since the earliest times, geometry has been inseparable from magic. Even the most archaic rock-scribings are geometrical in form. These hint at a notational and invocational system practised by some ancient priesthood. Because the complexities and abstract truths expressed by geometrical form could only be explained as reflections of the innermost truths of the world's being, they were held to be sacred mysteries of the highest order and were shielded from the eyes of the profane. Specialist knowledge was required to draw such figures, and their mystic importance was unheeded by the untutored masses. Complex concepts could be transmitted from one initiate to another by means of individual geometrical symbols or combinations of them without the ignorant even realising that any communication had taken place. Like the modern system of secret symbols employed by

Sacred Geometry

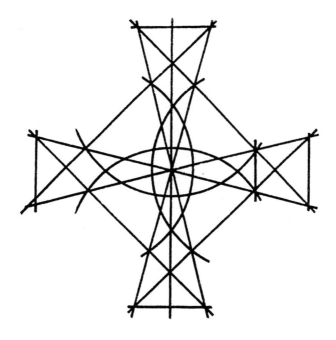

2. The Polynesian Mattang, the mnemonic geometry inherent in wave patterns.

gypsies, at best they would be puzzling enigmas to the curious.

Each geometrical form is invested with psychological and symbolic meaning. Thus anything made by the hands of men which incorporates these symbols in some way or other becomes a vehicle for the ideas and conceptions embodied in its geometry. Through the ages, complex symbolic geometries have acted as the bases for sacred and profane architecture, the geometry varying according to the function. Some geometries remain today as potent archetypal images of faith: the hexagram as the symbol of Judaism springs to mind. Other geometries have remained less overt, being used to indicate to those 'in the know' some esoteric truth, like the vesica piscis on the lid of the Chalice Well at Glastonbury. Yet

The Principles of Sacred Geometry

others lie hidden in the depths of mystical artworks - or even in the games of children.

3. The lid of the Chalice Well, Glastonbury, showing the Vesica Piscis. Designed by Frederick Bligh Bond.

One game common among schoolchildren is a remnant of an ancient system of sacred geometry. Known as 'fortune telling', the game involves folding a square of paper in a certain way. This enables the paper to be opened at will to disclose one of four choices. The folding of the paper and the form it takes when unfolded again is a ready mnemonic for creating the ad quadratum geometry used by the old masons.

A square of paper is taken and the four corners are folded to meet one another. This produces a square whose area is half that of the original. These corners are again folded from the back, which creates another square half the size of the former, making an eightfold division. From this, a three-dimensional figure can be made, with two groups of opposing 'cusps' which can be opened and shut at will. The association of this precisely- defined geometry with fortune telling may well be the degenerate remnant of an ancient system of divination, for the pattern thus formed not only reproduces the basic configuration for ad quadra turn, but also the traditional layout for drawing the horoscope. This latter pattern combines in an ingenious way the pagan eightfold division of the square with the Eastern twelvefold division of the zodiac.

The use of geometrical forms is well known in ritual magic, both for the evocation of spirits and powers and for the protection of the magician from their malevolent attentions. Each spirit has traditionally a sigil or geometrical pattern associated with its name, by which means, with the appropriate spells and ritual, it may be contacted. Many of these sigils are geometrical expressions of the names, produced by plotting out number equivalents of letters on magic squares. The determination of number equivalents to names is known as gematria. In the Greek and Hebrew alphabets, each character stands not only for a sound but also for a numerical equivalent. Thus the name Israel would be written in Hebrew: Yod Shin Resh Aleph Lamed. These characters have the numerical equivalent: 10, 300, 200, 1, 30 = 541. In gematria, the convention then allows other words of equivalent numerical value to be used as substitutes. Qabalists over the centuries have studied the hidden meaning of the book of Isaiah in this way. Substituting one word for another can be used as an occult method of communication which obviates the necessity for using the actual name, which has its own special powers. The numbers themselves can also be plotted as positions on magic squares. Thus, our example, Israel, plotted on the Magic Square of the Sun, creates a specific sigil which may then be transferred to magical utensils, etc (see Figure 4).

6	32	3	34	35	1
7	11	27	28	8	30
19	14	16	15	23	24
18	20	22	21	17	13
25	29	10	9	26	12
36	5	33	4	2	31

4. The sigil of 'Israel' projected onto the magic square of the Sun.

Wherever geometry has been used, whether consciously or unconsciously, its symbolism still functions. Throughout the known universe the function of this geometry is an unchanging value in transitory existence. Artists and magicians alike have recognised this transcendental quality and it has consequently formed the changeless basis upon

Sacred Geometry

which the fabric of culture is hung. Throughout recorded history, the geometrician has been quietly working at his craft, providing the inner matrix upon which the outward forms are based.

2. The Forms

There are but a few basic geometrical forms from which all of the diversity of structure in the universe is composed. Each form is endowed with its own unique properties, and carries an esoteric symbolism which has remained unchanged throughout human history.

All of these basic geometrical forms may be generated easily by means of the two tools which geometers have used since the dawn of history - the straightedge and compasses. As universal figures, their construction requires no use of any measurement; they occur throughout natural formations, both in the organic and inorganic kingdoms.

The Circle

The circle was perhaps the earliest of the symbols drawn by the human race. Simple to draw, it is an everyday form visible in nature, seen in the heavens as the discs of sun and moon, occurring in the forms of plants and animals and in natural geological structures. In the earliest times, buildings, whether temporary or permanent, were mostly circular. The Native American tipi and the Mongolian yurt of today are but survivals of a universal earlier form. From the hut circles of Neolithic Britain, through the megalithic stone circles to round churches and temples, the circular form has imitated the roundness of the visible horizon, making each building in effect a little world in itself.

The circle represents completion and wholeness, and round structures peculiarly echo this principle. In the ancient alchemical treatise, the Rosarium Philosophorum, we read:

> Make a round circle of the man and the woman, and draw out of this a square, and out of the square a triangle. Make a round circle and you will have the stone of the philosophers.

The circle is here portrayed as encompassing the image of man, as in the famous Vitruvian drawing by Leonardo da Vinci. From this fundamental figure, the square may be produced, and thence the other geometrical figures. The stone of the philosophers, the sum of all things and the key to knowledge, is thus reproduced and represented by the circle, the mother figure from which all other geometrical figures may be generated. With straightedge and compasses, all the major figures were simply and elegantly produced. These figures, the vesica piscis, equilateral triangle, square, hexagon and pentagon, all carry within themselves direct relationships with one another.

The Square

Early temples were often built foursquare. Representing the microcosm, and hence emblematical of the stability of the world, this characteristic was especially true of the artificial world- mountains, the ziggurats, pyramids and stupas. These structures symbolised the transition-point between heaven and earth and were ideally centred at the omphalos, the axial point at the centre of the world.

The Forms

Geometrically, the square is a unique figure. It is capable of precise division by two and multiples of two by drawing only. It may be divided into four squares by making a cross which automatically defines the exact centre of the square. The square, oriented towards the four cardinal points (in the case of the Egyptian pyramids, with phenomenal accuracy), may be again bisected by diagonals, dividing it into eight triangles.

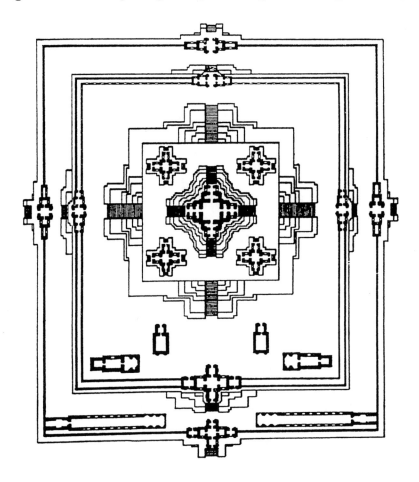

5. The Takéo, Angkor Thom, Cambodia, a temple based upon the square, Ground plan.

These eight lines, radiating from the centre, form the axes towards the four cardinal directions, and the 'four corners' of the world - the eightfold division of space.

This eightfold division of space is enshrined in the 'eightfold path' of the Buddhist religion, and the 'Four Royal Roads of Britain' recounted in the History of the Kings of Britain by Geoffrey of Monmouth. Each of the eight directions in Tibet were under the hereditary symbolic guardianship of a family, a tradition which was paralleled in Britain in the eight Noble Families which survived Christianization to produce the kings and saints of the Celtic Church.

The eightfold division of the square was, in the European tradition, emblematical of the division of the day and year as well as the division of the country and society. Although the eightfold division of time was gradually eliminated with the advent of the Christians' twelvefold system, it survived in the old 'quarterdays' of the calendar, the traditional fire festivals of country pagans, and the masonic geometry of sacred architecture in the system *acht uhr* or *ad quadratum*. I will return to this important matter in a later chapter.

The Hexagon

The hexagon is a natural geometrical figure produced by the division of the circumference of a circle by its radius. The points on the circumference are connected by straight lines, making a figure with six equal sides.

Being a function of the relationship between the radius and circumference of the circle, the hexagon is a natural figure which occurs throughout nature. It is produced naturally in the boiling and mixing of liquids. The French physicist Bénard noted that during his experiments on diffusion in liquids, hexagonal patterns were often formed on the surface. Such

The Forms

tourbillons cellulaires, or 'Bénard cells', were the subject of many experiments. It was found that under conditions of perfect equilibrium the patterns would form perfect hexagons. These patterns were likened to those of the cells which make up organic life, or the prismatic forms of basalt rocks. Being subject to the same universal forces of viscosity and diffusion, similar patterns are naturally created in a simmering liquid.

The best-known natural hexagon can be seen in the bees' honeycomb. This is composed of an assemblage of hexagonal prisms whose precision is so astonishing that it has attracted the attention of many philosophers, who have seen in it a manifestation of the divine harmony in nature. In antiquity, Pappus the Alexandrine devoted his attentions to this hexagonal plan and came to the conclusion that the bees were endowed with a 'certain geometrical forethought', with economy as the guiding principle, 'there being, then, three figures which of themselves can fill up the space round a point, namely, the triangle, the square and the hexagon, the bees have wisely selected for their structure that which contains most angles, suspecting indeed that it could hold more honey than either of the other two.

In my own researches into the structure of marine micro-organisms, I have found the hexagon in the external form of a North American marine alga *Pyramimonas virginica*. Here, the bases of the structures which cover the organism's body form perfect hexagons, though they are smaller than the wavelength of visible light. This natural geometry, of which the Roman author Pliny tells us men made a life's work of studying even in his time, is of especial interest to the mystic geometer.

The hexagon's direct relationship to the circle is allied to another interesting property in which the alternate vertices of the figure are joined by straight lines to produce the hexagram. This figure, composed of interpenetrating equilateral triangles, symbolises the fusion of opposing principles: male and female, hot and cold, water an fire, earth and air, etc., and is consequently symbolic of the archetypal whole, the divine power of creation. Thus, it was used in alchemy and remains the sacred symbol of the Jews to this day. The dimensions of the triangles which form the hexagram are directly related to the circle which produces them, and can be made the starting point for geometrical developments.

The Vesica Piscis, the Triangle and the Platonic Solids

The vesica piscis is that figure produced when two circles of equal size are drawn through each others' centres. In sacred geometrical terms, it is the derivation-point of the equilateral triangle and straight-line geometry from the circle. It has represented the genitals of the Mother Goddess, the physical springing-point of life symbolised by its fundamental position in geometry. Likewise, it has played a prime position in the foundation of holy buildings. From the earliest stone circles and temples to the great cathedrals of the medieval period, the initial act of foundation has been related to the sunrise on a preordained day. This symbolic birth of the temple with the new sun is a universal theme, and its connexion with the genital-like vesica is no accident. The geometry of the Hindu temple, like that of its spiritual counterparts in Asia Minor, North Africa or Europe, is recorded as being derived directly from the shadow of an upright or gnomon. The ancient Sanskrit text on temple foundation, the Manasara Shilna Shastra, details the derivation of plan from orientation.

The site having been chosen by a practitioner of geomancy, an upright was thrust into the ground at that point. A circle was drawn around it. This procedure gives a true east- west axis. From each end of this axis, arcs were drawn, producing a vesica piscis which in turn gave a north-south axis. Thus, the universal vesica was fundamental in the temple's foundation. From this initial vesica, another at right angles was drawn and from this a central circle and thence a square directed to the four quarters of the earth. This Hindu system of foundation may be seen as fundamentally identical to that used in the Roman method of city foundation and layout described in the works of Vitruvius. It is produced directly by observation and as such reproduces the conditions prevalent at the precise moment of the foundation. This fixing in time, like the moment of birth in astrology, is fundamental in all practices of orientation, as such an alignment automatically embodies the astronomical and hence astrological attributes of the time. In addition to this, the place s geomantic characteristics, which set it aside as something unique, are incorporated in the temple.

The vesica is not involved in foundation through arbitrary principles. It is the practical point of departure from which all other geometrical figures may be derived. Dividing by a line across its width with lines connected thence to the vertices produces the rhombus, formed of two equilateral triangles base to base. The sides of these triangles are equal in length to the radius of the generating circle. From the equilateral triangle, the hexagon and the icosahedron may easily be generated. In esoteric terms, the whole series of regular geometric solids known universally as the Platonic Solids may be generated from plane figures.

In the Timaeus, Plato wrote, 'Now the one [triangle] which we maintain to be the most beautiful of all the many triangles (we need not speak of the others) is that of which the double forms a third triangle which is equilateral ... then let us choose two triangles, out of which fire and the other elements have been constructed, one isosceles, the other having the square of the longer side equal to three times the square of the lesser side.' In Plato's system, geometrical symbolism was held

Sacred Geometry

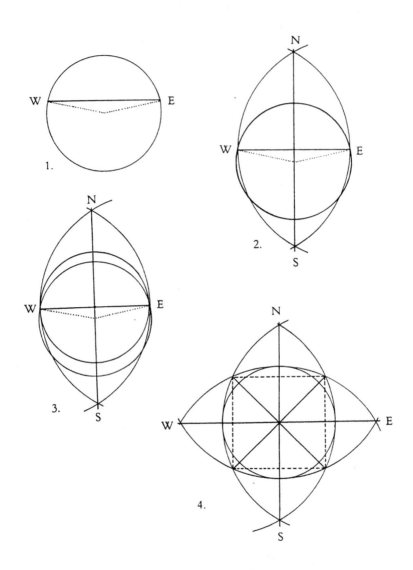

6. Laying out the temple, from te Manasara Shilpa Shastra, 1: The east-west line, 2: the north-south versica, 3: producing the quartered circle, 4: the double versica and square.

to account for all known states of matter. Especially important was the series of solid figures which was the essence of this philosophy. By occult means, the whole series was symbolised by a figure now sported by Freemasons of the Holy Royal Arch grade. This symbol is the equilateral triangle enclosed within a hexagram. Its symbolism is 'resolved' by adding together the values of the angles made by the various parts, and breaking into however many right angles that value equals. This arcane method enables any geometrical figure to be 'resolved' and thus infuses its simplicity with a rich symbolism which has been exploited to the full by architects of sacred buildings.

The equilateral triangle resolved into the tetrahedron is equal in geometrical value to eight right angles - the number of degrees in four equilateral triangles. On account of its being the smallest regular geometrical solid, and because of its pyramidal form, it was used by the Platonists to represent the element fire.

The 'resolved' triangles in the hexagram or Solomon's Seal, without taking into account the intersections (which are conventionally shown as interlaces rather than junctions), are equivalent to sixteen right angles. This is the number contained in the octahedron, the Platonic solid composed of eight equal- sized equilateral triangles. This was ascribed by the Platonists to the element air, being next in lightness to the tetrahedron.

Ignoring the intersections, Solomon's Seal with its superimposed smaller triangle will resolve into the number of degrees found in twenty-four angles. This is the number found in the cube, a solid composed of six equal squares. This solid and immovable figure symbolised to the Platonists the element earth. It has universally represented this element wherever it has occurred in sacred geometry - the foursquare basis of the temple and the Holy City, immovably implanted above the omphalos.

Sacred Geometry

7. The Platonic solids' sigil: equilateral triangle inside Solomon's Seal.

The inverted triangle of the seal with the enclosed smaller triangle, added to the upright larger triangle of the hexagram resolve as forty right angles, equal in degrees to those found in the icosahedron, a regular bounded by twenty equal-sized equilateral triangles. This is the heaviest regular solid bounded by triangles. Next in heaviness from the cube, the icosahedron represented the element water. Thus, any form derived from the hexagram with its internal triangle is seen as embodying all the Platonic Solids and thus by association the four elements - an attribute of universality, and a symbol of the law of the unity of opposites.

The Golden Section

The Golden Section is a ratio which has been used in sophisticated artwork and in sacred architecture from the period of ancient Egypt. In ancient Egypt and Greece, there occurred an extensive use of what the early twentieth-century geometrician Jay Hambridge dubbed 'dynamic symmetry'. Both Egyptian and Greek sacred objects and buildings have geometries based upon the division of space attained by the root rectangles and their derivatives. The root rectangles are produced directly from the square by simple drawing with compasses, and thus come into the category of classical geometry, produced without measurement.

A whole connected series of root rectangles exists. The first of the root rectangles is the square, which is a 'root 1' rectangle. The next, the √2 rectangle, is produced from the square by the

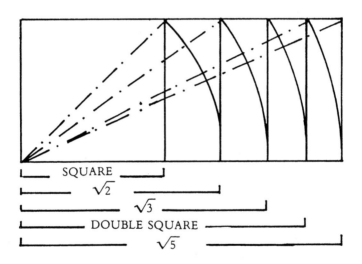

8. The 'root' rectangles and their production.

simple expedient of setting the compasses at the length of the diagonal and producing the base line to meet it. This makes the length of the long side equal to the square root of 2, taking the short side as unity. The √3 rectangle is produced from the diagonal of this rectangle, and so on.

Although the sides of these rectangles are not measurable in terms of number, the Greeks said that such lines were not really irrational because they were measurable in terms of the squares produced from them. Measurability in terms of square area instead of length was the great secret of ancient Greek sacred geometry. The famous theorem of Pythagoras, known to every schoolchild, is understandable only in terms of square measure. For instance, the relationship between the end and side of a √5 rectangle is a relationship of area, because the square constructed on the end of a √5 rectangle is exactly one fifth of the area of a square constructed on its side. Such rectangles possess a property which enables them to be divided into many smaller shapes which are also measurable parts of the whole.

This brings us to another fundamental factor in the design of sacred architecture: proportion, and its siamese twin, commensurability. Music demonstrates this admirably in its harmonies, and indeed it has been said that music is in reality geometry translated into sound, for in music the same harmonies can be heard which underlie architectural proportion. Commensurability, which ensures complete harmony throughout a building or work of art, is a rational integration of all the proportions of all the parts of a building in such a way that every part has its absolutely fixed shape and size. Nothing could be added to or removed from such a harmonious ensemble without disrupting the harmony of the whole. Certain rectangles which are the starting-point for related geometrical figures commonly form the bases for such harmonising patterns.

Rectangles with side-to-side ratios of 3:2, 5:4, 8:5, 13:6, etc., in which the proportions are expressed in whole numbers, have been given the name static rectangles. Rectangles like the root rectangles have been dubbed dynamic rectangles. These later rectangles are more often encountered in geometrical composition. They allow a much greater flexibility in use than the static rectangles, especially when used in order to establish the harmony of the elements by proportion.

There are a few rectangles which combine the features of the static and the dynamic. These are the square and the double square ($1 = 1:1 = \sqrt{1}:1$ and $2 = 2:1\ \sqrt{4}:1$). The diagonal of the double square, which is perhaps the most favoured form for sacred enclosures, is $\sqrt{5}$. This irrational number directly relates the root 2 or root 4 rectangle to the root 5 rectangle, which is directly related to the golden section proportion:

$$\frac{\sqrt{5}+1}{2}$$

This important ratio, called the Section by the ancient Greeks, the Divine Proportion by Luca Pacioli (1509), and dubbed by Leonardo and his followers the Golden Section, has unique properties which have commended it to geometers since Egyptian times.

The Golden Section exists between two measurable quantities of any kind when the ratio between the larger and the smaller one is equal to the ratio between the sum of the two and the larger one. In geometrical terms, it may be easily generated from the double square. If one of the two squares is cut in half, and the diagonal of this half is swung down to the base, the place at which it cuts the base will be 1.618 units in relation to the side of the square which is 1 unit in length. The ratio may also be generated from the pentagram and its associated pentagon, where the ratio between the side of the pentagon and its extension into the pentagram fulfils the equation:

$$\frac{\sqrt{5}+1}{2} = 1.618$$

This is symbolised in geometrical convention2 by the Greek letter ϕ. Numerically, it possesses exceptional algebraical, mathematical and geometrical properties. $\phi = 1.618$; $\phi = 0.618$ and $\phi^2 = 2.618$. In any increasing progression or series of terms having ϕ as the ratio between the successive terms, each term is equal to the sum of the two preceding ones. This unique property permits a simple manipulation of a whole series. From any two successive terms, all others may be constructed by simple moves of the compass.

In numerical terms, this additive series was first popularised in Europe by Leonardo Bigollo Fibonacci, otherwise known as Leonardo da Pisa. Born in 1179, Leonardo travelled with his father to Algiers, where, from Arab geometers he learnt the secret of the series, and from whence he was able to introduce Arabic numerals into Europe. Both concepts revolutionised European mathematics.

This numerical series, which is now known by the name of the Fibonacci Series, has long been recognised as a principle occurring in the structure of living organisms, and thus as a principle inherent in the structure of the world. Its construction is deceptively simple: the next term is the sum of the two previous terms, i.e., 1, 2, 3, 5, 8, 13, 21, 34, 55, 89, 144, and soon. The arrangement of leaves on a plant, the pads on a cat's foot, the spirals encountered in the shells of microscopic formainifera, are all governed by the Fibonacci series.

The Golden Section has been honoured throughout history. Plato, in his Timaeus discussed it as the key to the physics of the cosmos. Luca Pacioli, the Renaissance geometrician, published the influential work De Divina Proportione at Venice in 1509, and even the modern architect Le Corbusier, father of the tower block, devised a modular system of proportion based upon this ancient but potent ratio.

3. Ancient British Geometry

Prechristian sacred and cultural structures can be understood only by adopting the viewpoint of the ancients. For them everything mundane was bound up with the divine. All human thoughts and actions were subordinated to the energising influences of the all- powerful divine forces. Their philosophy and wisdom culminated in the knowledge that 'as above, so below', and in the attempt to bring all their activities and ambitions into harmony with higher nature, the Divine Will.

Josef Heinsch

All over the British Isles and Northern Europe are the last remnants of a long-lost culture: standing stones. Rugged reminders of an age almost unimaginably distant, the megaliths of Europe still survive in considerable numbers. Although perhaps the majority have disappeared in the 3-5,000 years since they were erected, several sites still survive virtually intact. Some of these enigmatic megaliths are solitary and unhewn; others are arranged into complex formations. Yet others have been dressed, and bear carvings both figurative and abstract.

Some of the most archaic and enigmatic of ancient rock carvings which survive to this day are the cup- and ring markings which may be found on standing stones and less

Ancient British Geometry

commonly on natural outcrops of rock. For several hundred years they have been the sources of legend, the object of veneration for the superstitious and the subject of comment and speculation from local antiquaries. Many scholarly commentators have ventured their theses over their function and meaning, yet they remain an outstanding puzzle in prehistoric research.

Their designs are diverse, being rarely repeated, placed upon the stone without any obvious order. Cup- and ring-marks consist of small cup-like depressions in the rock, mainly

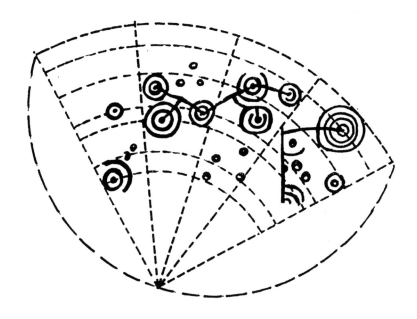

9. Drumtrodden rock sculpturings. After *Archaic Sculpturings*, (1915) by L. MacLellan Mann.

circular, but occasionally oval in form. Often these 'cups' are surrounded by concentric rings. These are sometimes eccentric or even penannular. They vary in number, and may be associated with radial lines which cut through the rings and sometimes link the cup-ring system to another on a different part of the rock surface. Spirals are rare, as are ladder-like engravings. In Ireland designs like stars or sun wheels with radiating lines are common. These parallel some of the hieroglyph in the ancient Scandinavian rock-scribings known as hällristningar, which were the forerunners of runic characters. Although such petroglyphs range across Europe into Asia, local variations are often sufficient to distinguish one locality's marks from another.

Numerous conjectures have been advanced for the meaning of cup- and ring-markings. Authors have classed them as tribal territory-markers, charts of prehistoric villages with their pathways, genealogical 'trees', a kind of undeciphered writing, channels for sacrificial blood, charts of the positions of standing stones, or figurative houses of the dead.

One of the few systematic studies on the meaning of these inscrutable signs was carried out by the Scottish antiquary Ludovic MacLellan Mann, an independent-minded researcher whose work is little known today. In 1915, he published Archaic Sculpturings in which he collated the results of a number of years of research into ancient rock- carvings. After analysis, MacLellan Mann had arrived at the conclusion that cup- and ring- markings were part of a coherent system. In Archaic Sculpturings, MacLellan Mann wrote:

> Some years ago ... I began to make an examination of many dozens of groups of these markings, and much to my astonishment I found that, instead of the markings being all higgledy-piggledy, they were arranged in a most precise, mathematical, and geometrical manner ... While these sculpturings present markedly different

types, they have all been laid down with the same ideas and under the same system. I have observed that straight lines can be drawn through certain essential parts, such as along the often straightly set gutters, or through the centres of three or more cups or sets of penannular rings. These lines when produced were found to converge and meet precisely at common focal points well beyond the field of the sculpturings... Round each of these foci will be found to be disposed a set of concentric zones, into many of which fit the main or essential parts of the sculptured work, so accurately and frequently as to point to some factor being at work which is not chance, accident or coincidence.

Mann's analysis of the underlying geometry which he discovered in cup- and ring-marks was interpreted in astronomical terms. There were two main centres which determined the markings by the radial and concentric zones generated from them. One centre, MacLellan Mann believed, was often cut by a line which represented a precise north-south, and through the other centre ran a northerly-southerly line two to four degrees divergent in direction. Thus, two complementary systems of lines fitted into the salient parts of the carving. One was related to terrestrial north - the actual pole of the planet earth - whilst the other was determined by the position of the pole star or magnetic north at the time. MacLellan Mann believed that his radial grid within which the actual carvings were made was a reference system which showed the positions of heavenly bodies at certain moments during the year. Such astronomical marker carvings have been found on every continent. Dating back as much as 30,000 years, they are the product of pre- literate, but not preastronomical, societies.

The facts of astronomy were slowly accumulated through centuries of direct observation and record, which need not

Sacred Geometry

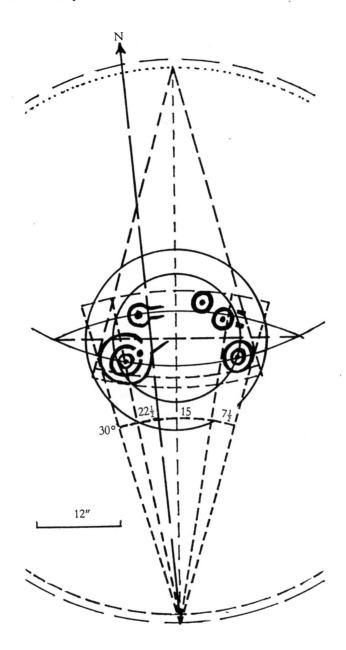

10. Kirkcudbright sculpturings. After *Archaic Sculpturings*.

have involved the use of writing as we know it. The secrets of geometry were arrived at by trial and error, and the expediency of the observation of the stars. Having developed the function of calendar-making, and hence the record of celestial activity, the early priesthoods which organised such matters needed some method of determining the precise time of year for the performance of each of their practical and ritual observances.

The fundamental necessity of determining the precise times at which magical or religious rites are to be performed is demonstrated at the present day in the rituals of the North American Hopi tribe. At certain times of the year, the priests and members of the religious societies descend into their Kivas (subterranean shrines) and watch the stars through the vertical entrance. Various appropriate songs and actions are performed during the time which the important constellations take to pass overhead. The duration of the whole ceremony is thus determined by the passing of the stars. In this way, the rites are harmonised by direct observation with the prevailing astronomical and astrological conditions.

Something similar must have been the motivation of those who built the megalithic observatories of Europe. The only way they could do this was to construct observation points which precisely measured and defined the passage of time. This necessity led to the discovery that the cycles of sun-, moon- and star-rise and set are not at all subject to simple laws.

This gradual awakening in understanding is reflected in the remains of the megalithic culture in Britain, where archaeology has shown that the stone and wood observatories were rebuilt at intervals. Each rebuilding incorporated progressive increases in complexity and sophistication. The construction of more and more complex an accurate observatories went hand-in-hand with the invention and employment of increasingly complex geometries. Considerable knowledge and expertise were required for the design, planning and construction of such a vast undertaking as Stonehenge. To find the correct site for the observation of celestial phenomena and the erection there of large standing stones which accurately marked the passage of the heavens relied heavily upon an accurate science of applied geometry.

MacLellan Mann found that this had indeed existed. The underlying geometry he had detected in the cup- and ring-marks could also be found on a much larger scale. 'The late Neolithic architect', wrote MacLellan Mann in Archaic Sculpturings, 'when laying down, for example, the ground plan of the horned cairns of Caithness, possessed these same curious notions. I have worked out his ground plans carefully, and they show, just like the rock- cuttings, the arc of the circle represented by the side structures, and the curve of an ellipse at each end of the monument ... the apparently isolated cairns, the groups of standing stones far distant from each other, and the detached sets of rock carvings well removed from each other, may all form part of one widely spread design.'

In 1937, during excavations for sand at Knappers, seven miles from the city of Glasgow, the remains of the foundations of an ancient wooden temple were discovered. These remains were brought to MacLellan Mann's attention. He analyzed them and their associated serpentine palisading and found that their design was comparable on a massive scale with the cup- and ring-marks he had studied.

In *The Druids' Temple near Glasgow*, published in 1937, MacLellan Mann wrote: The layout of the whole area is systematic and precise. By interpreting the linear and angular dimensions into astronomical recurrent periods, each serpent figure can be identified from the length of its medial line with one or other of the heavenly bodies - the Sun, the Moon, and the five planets, or with the evil spirit of the Eclipse Year. The

Ancient British Geometry

various circular palisadings are found to represent the main astronomical periods such as the luni-solar cycle of 19 years or the Saros Cycle, of 18 years 101 days, at the end of which eclipses may occur.

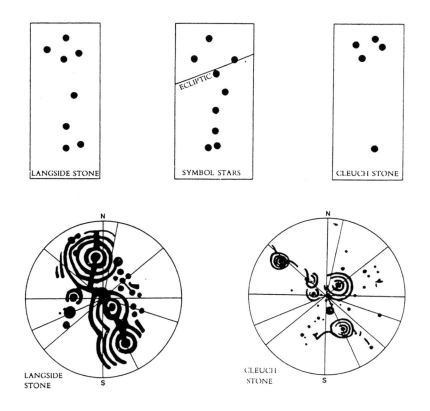

11. The relationship of star patterns with cup-and-ring-marks.

The 'Druids' Temple' was the subject of an appeal, but the advent of the Second World War prevented any preservation. In MacLellan Mann's day, however, because of lack of resources, accurate surveys and analyses of ancient structures

Sacred Geometry

were not carried out in great numbers. Until Professor Thorn's studies, which have involved him personally in the accurate survey of hundreds of megalithic sites in the British Isles and in Brittany, sentiments like those expressed by MacLellan Mann could be dismissed by the conservative-minded as fanciful. The eccentric shapes which are apparent in most stone 'circles' were commonly held to be attributable to the incompetence of their builders, who were, by the scientists of the Victorian school, envisaged as savages of low intellect, scarcely higher than the apes. Common sense tells us, however, that technicians who could transport large stones over considerable distances (e.g. the bluestones from Mynydd Preseli in Wales to Stonehenge) would find it easy to lay out a true circle.

However, the geometries required to construct observatories for the study and documentation of the variable phenomena of the heavens are far more complex than could be accommodated by a simple circle. Thus, more complex forms were utilised.

The great megalithic ensembles of ancient Britain, and indeed the lesser stone circles which dot the moors and uninhabited parts of the country, were conclusively demonstrated by Professor Thorn to have been laid out with astounding precision. This precise geometry involved the use of integral right-angled triangles ('Pythagorean' triangles) laid out to a remarkably constant measure - 2.72 feet - which Thorn dubbed the megalithic Yard (MY).

The eccentric stone circles, far from being symptomatic of their builders' failure in technique, were actually constructed according to specific ground rules, based upon integral triangles. Thom's Type 1 'circles' are in fact egg -shaped rings, base on two 3:4:5 right-angled triangles place back to back. Another common 'circle', Type 2, is again based on two 3:4:5 triangles, but this time with a common hypotenuse. Other,

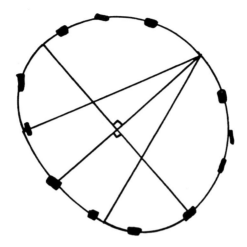

12. Plan of Barbrook 1 stone circle, Derbyshire. A 'flattened type B' geometry. Four arcs based on geometrically-defined centres.

more complex, arrangements, Thom found, were produced from other integral right-angled triangles such as 5:12:13 or 8:15:17. Stonehenge is a complex amalgam of circles and perfect ellipses, and is also analysable in conventional geometry.

MacLellan Mann's researches and later Thom's complementary discoveries of sighting lines from stone circles to the horizon or other markers for the purpose of celestial observation and record show the next stage of development from the microcosmic to the macrocosmic. Early this century, Boyle Somerville and Sir Norman Lockyer had noted such alignments, but until Thorn's exhaustive studies, they had remained at best hypothetical.

Sacred Geometry

Lockyer is best known for his work at and around Stonehenge, the district later studied by the German school of geomantic research. During his enquiries, he discovered that the well-known midsummer sunrise line which is marked at Stonehenge by the famous Heelstone, was actually just a small part of a longer alignment of ancient sites. On surveying the avenue which marks the position of sunrise on the longest day of the year when viewed from the centre of the circle, Lockyer noted that it was in line with the ancient earthwork at Silbury Hill. When extended in the opposite direction, this line was found to align upon Grovely Castle and Castle Ditches, also ancient earth works. This alignment had previously been noted by Colonel Johnstone, then Director General of the Ordnance Survey. The line had been used in an improved survey of the district, which led to an increase in the accuracy of Ordnance Survey maps.

The section between Grovely Castle and Stonehenge, which is almost exactly six miles in length, was found by Lockyer to form one side of an equilateral triangle whose apex is at the site of the ancient city of Old Sarum, also an ancient earthwork. Old Sarum is on the alignment Stonehenge-Old Sarum-Salisbury Cathedral-Clearbury Ring- Frankenbury. Thus, the layout of Stonehenge, whose geometry was designed according to celestial factors, is integrated with the artificial landscape geometry of the country, at one with the positions of other ancient earthworks, defined by and defining their placement.

Stonehenge combines several geometries within one masterful scheme. Related both to heavenly phenomena and to the surrounding countryside, it is sited at a key geomantic point with regard to the overall landscape geometry of southern England. The henge is sited on several important ley lines, including one which runs from St Michael's church tower which stands atop Glastonbury Tor. This ley, which comes from Glastonbury Tor via St Michael's, Gare Hill, Maiden

Ancient British Geometry

Bradley Priory, Stonehenge, and Shere Church to a tumulus in Deerleap Wood near Dorking in Surrey, is, like the sunrise line at Stonehenge, an extension of the side of a geometrical figure of vast dimensions. In this case, it is the extension of the side of a decagon which links vital geomantic points with one another.

The geometry of the henge itself, based upon the solsticial axis, shows a tendency towards a sixfold division. This has been noted since the time of Inigo Jones (1652) and has evoked comments from mystics such as John Wood, Herman Gaylord Wood and John Michael. Lockyer's discovery of an equilateral triangle with six-mile sides links the microcosmic sixfold sacred geometry with macrocosmic landscape geometry.

Lockyer, however, was but one in a long line of researchers who have studied the alignment of ancient sites. Between 1870 and 1872, an expert on Roman roads named William Henry Black made public a startling theory. He had pursued his studies for fifty years before unleashing the results on an unsuspecting and unbelieving public. Black claimed that he had uncovered nothing less than a whole system of 'grand geometric lines', radial and polygonal, which ran across the whole of Britain and beyond. They linked major landmarks in a precise manner, even defining the boundary-markers of counties.

Such a concept had never before been given currency. Apart from a reference in an obscure occult book published in 1846 to a line of ancient earth works in Wiltshire, even alignments had not been countenanced.

Black died in 1872, but no followers elaborated or even corroborated his findings. However, he was not without influence. His major talk on 'grand geometric lines' was given at Hereford in 1870 during a field trip of the British

Archaeological Association. The meeting at which Black spoke was chaired by a local worthy, Dr Bull of the Woolhope Naturalists' Club. In the years following Black's death, Bull publicly mentioned his work on several occasions. At one such meeting was a local flour miller and photographic pioneer with an interest in antiquities - Alfred Watkins.

Fifty years after Black spoke in Hereford, Watkins announced that he had made a momentous discovery - alignments of ancient sites, to which he gave the name of 'leys'. Watkins, like Black and others before him, had found that ancient earthworks, boundary markers, churches and other classes of ancient monument were arranged in straight lines. Through his books Early British Trackways, The Old Straight Track and Archaic Tracks Around Cambridge, Watkins became the best-known exponent of aligned sites, the father of the 'ley hunters' as his followers are known. Unlike Black, who thought his grand geometrical lines were the remains of an ancient survey, Watkins felt that his alignments were the remnants of an ancient network of trackways.

Watkins only scratched the surface of oriented alignments, and the relationship of radial centres to geometry was not touched upon. This is strange, as Watkins had certainly heard of Black and must have known the work of MacLellan Mann, who had mentioned 'stones ... in an exact geometrical relationship'. As it is, Watkins devoted his later life to disseminating his ideas on alignments. Although he died as long ago as 1935, it is only in the last fifteen years that his work has become well known and in- depth studies based upon it, especially those by Paul Devereux and Ian Thomson, have verified many of his findings.

Watkins and his school largely ignored the work of Lockyer, who had a much greater impact in Germany than in his native Britain. Shortly after the publication of his book Stonehenge and Other British Stone Monuments Astronomically

Considered (1909), a German surveyor named Albrecht published a discussion of the astronomical significance of Stonehenge in the periodical Das Weltall (The Universe). His initial source was Lockyer. Shortly afterwards, Albrecht was killed in the Great War, but in 1920, Father Leugering read his work and began to search for similar systems in his native Westphalia.

The defeated Germany of the 1920s was fertile ground for revolutionary and chauvinistic sentiments, and students of 'sacred geography' as it was known found their niche. Leugering's collaborator, Josef Heinsch, a lawyer and regional planner, discovered Stonehenge-type alignments all over Germany. In his researches, he studied both sacred geography and the microcosmic aspect, sacred geometry, which he showed to be two aspects of the same geomantic discipline.

The main champion of ancient Germanic culture was Wilhelm Teudt, who above all others was to become the figurehead of the science of landscape geometry. In his major book *Germanische Heilitümer* (Ancient German Sanctuaries), published in 1929, he announced his discovery of alignments which he called heilige linien (holy lines). These, he found, were sighted on astronomical phenomena. In the Teutoburger Wald, the mystical heartland of Germany, the site of so many legendary and heroic deeds, Teudt studied the orientations of the irregularly hexagonal earthworks at the Haus Gierke at Oesterholz. These earth works were situated around a hunting lodge of the seventeenth century, yet Teudt claimed that the earthworks themselves were the remains of an ancient astronomical observatory. The earthworks' orientations were checked by professional astronomers and were found to be aligned upon several major astronomical features in their positions in 1800 B.C. Heinsch begged to differ, stating that the earthworks' forms, whilst ancient, were determined by simple sacred geometry.

Sacred Geometry

Teudt's heilige linien, which linked significant sites, although primarily astronomical, were similar in concept to Black's geometrical lines and Watkins's leys. From any major ancient earthwork, Teudt found that there would be at least one orientation marker in the form of a so-called 'watch tower' along the north-south or east-west axis. The lines linked sacred sites in significant geometric relationships, being themselves linked to astronomical phenomena.

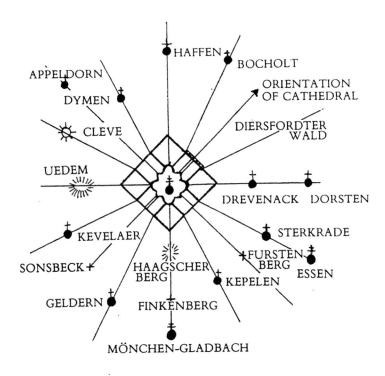

13. The landscape geometry around Xanten Cathedral, Germany. Josef Heinsch found that the mosaic discovered in the floor was orientated towards and contained the pattern of the layout of churches in the district.

By the late 1930s, the work of Teudt and his colleagues had been taken up by certain Nazis and given official patronage, which enabled the researchers to produce a large corpus of material on landscape geometry. Josef Heinsch discovered a vast interconnected system of alignments and geometrical figures with significant distances and angles which covered large sections of the Rhineland. Like previous geomantic researchers, he found that the geometry of the landscape was often a vastly enlarged version of the geometry of individual sites, making a physical link between microcosm and macrocosm. Heinsch saw his discovery as 'an almost indestructible sacred temple of nature', which was the continuum of sacred geometry in stone circles and temples with the layout of the landscape.

With the destruction of Nazi Germany, German geomantic researches all but ceased. The work of Teudt and his followers was all but forgotten until English geomantic researchers rediscovered it in the late 1970s. Much of the work of Heinsch and his colleagues has now been issued in English translation, and it has turned out to be some of the most detailed and convincing data yet collected.

A new generation of researchers is now studying landscape geometry. In his book *City of Revelation*, John Michael revealed the existence of a large-scale geometrical figure across southern Britain. The three ancient Celtic 'perpetual choirs' at Llantwit Major, Glastonbury Abbey and Stonehenge were shown to form three vertices of a regular decagon of majestic proportions. A fourth vertex exists at Goring-on-Thames where a major Pagan temple once stood at the junction of several important trackways. The centre of this vast decagon is at the hamlet of Whiteleaved Oak where the former counties of Hereford, Gloucester and Worcester came together. This decagon is related by angle and distance to the other major geomantic centres of Britain, and much work on such matters is now being undertaken.

Sacred Geometry

Researchers from Black to Michell have found the ancient patterns engraved almost indelibly into the landscape. The lines which crisscross the countryside are obviously of the same antiquity as the stone circles, yet the far more modern Christian churches and farm homesteads can almost invariably be fitted into the pattern. All such discoveries, both at the scale of stone scribings and circles and also across the whole breadth of the landscape, point to the existence of a former civilization, now utterly vanished, whose spiritual technology of geometry was unsurpassed. Its importance is indicated by the survival of its knowledge into the mystery schools of the late Middle Ages.

We can thus trace a progression in which the earliest rock scribings of unimaginable antiquity led with astronomy to the construction of complex and sophisticated stone observatories which themselves were linked together in an even larger geometric matrix. On the imposition of the Christian religion, these sites were often appropriated for churches. However, the orientations and positions were preserved, and the building's geometry was related directly to the earlier structure. Professor Lyle Borst has demonstrated in his book Megalithic Software that the geometrical patterns which underlie the easternmost chapels of the cathedrals at Wells, Lincoln, Canterbury, Gloucester, Winchester and several other places, are derived from Thorntype megalithic geometry and therefore indicate the former presence there of stone circles. In the cases of these Romanesque and Gothic cathedrals, the geometricians have synthesized the ancient megalithic geometry with the masonic ad triangulum and ad quadratum. The geometry of the heavens, translated into stone, was again transmuted to the service of other gods, yet it remains to this day recognisable to those who know what to look for.

4. Ancient Egyptian Sacred Geometry

Geometry literally means measuring the earth', and its development in ancient Egypt was precisely for that purpose. At a very early date, possibly five or six thousand years ago, the Egyptians developed an empirical scheme for surveying land. The basic scheme was born of necessity because the annual overflowing of the River Nile destroyed all boundaries. With the creation of centralised government, and in order to ensure an equitable taxation and to avoid disputes, boundaries had to be accurately re-established after each inundation. Of necessity, the method of surveying had to be practicable and simple. It required but two men and a knotted rope, and the knowledge of the so-called 'Pythagorean' triangle, centuries before Pythagoras walked this earth.

The laying out of areas required a foolproof method for the production of the right angle. This was achieved by marking off the rope with thirteen equal divisions. Four units then formed one side of the triangle, three another and five the hypotenuse opposite the right angle This simple method has persisted to this day, and was used when tomb and temple building began. It was the origin of the historic 'cording of the temple', and from this technique it was a relatively simple task to lay out rectangles and other more complex geometrical figures.

Sacred Geometry

As it developed the whole of ancient Egyptian culture became so infused with canonical religion that almost every act was formalised into an act of worship. The temples and tomb art are prime examples of this rigidly-organised sacred life. Complex magical ceremonies attended important state events in which the ruling monarch played a role as the personification of a deity. In the layout of temples, the basic formation of the underlying geometry was made into a complex symbolic ceremony.

In *The Dawn of Astronomy*, Sir Norman Lockyer noted that the cording of the temple', laying it out by means of the cord, was attended with a ceremonial comparable with the modern laying of a foundation-stone. He quotes descriptions of the process taken from wall-inscriptions at Edfu, Denderah and Karnak. 'Arose the king', says one of these inscriptions, 'attired in his necklace and feathered crown; and all the world followed him, and the majesty of Amenemhat. The ker-heb [High Priest read the sacred text during the stretching of the measuring cord and the laying of the foundation stone on the piece of ground selected for this temple. Then withdrew his majesty Amenemhat, and king Usertesen wrote it down before the people.'

The cord had a twofold function: to fix the orientation of the temple by direct observation of a celestial object; and also thence to lay out by simple geometry the sacred pattern of the temple itself. Another inscription reads: 'The living God, the magnificent son of Asti, nourished by the sublime goddess in the temple, the sovereign of the country, stretches the rope in joy, with his glance towards the ak of the Bull's Foreleg constellation, he establishes the temple-house of the mistress at Denderah, as took place there before.' This is a reference to the two temples of the Goddess at Denderah, one being sacred to Isis and the other to Hathor.

Ancient Egyptian Sacred Geometry

After the fixing of the orientation upon the constellation of the Bull's Foreleg (now known as The Plough or Ursa Major), the rope-fasteners found a line at right angles to it by means of creating a 3:4:5 triangle, and from that laid out the whole temple. Throughout recorded history, the rectangular form of the temple has been held to represent the body of man, and by microcosmic/macrocosmic correspondence, the heavens. Its complementary form, the central or radial geometrical pattern, equal in all directions and emblematical of the material world, in Egypt was admirably represented by the pyramids.

The construction of the pyramids was carried out over a relatively short period. Although some sixty pyramids are known, the largest and most celebrated of the group of three at Giza near Cairo has been the object of far more scrutiny

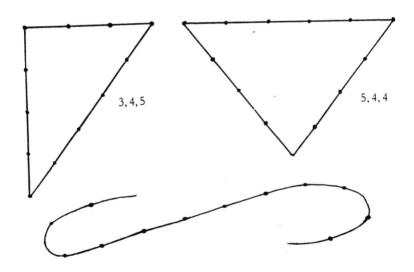

14. The 'Druids' Cord' - 13 sections with 12 knots, to produce the 3, 4, 5 triangle (right angle) and the 5, 4, 4 triangle (seventh part of a circle.

and speculation than any other. Testimony of ancient authors such as the fifth-century B.C. Greek Herodotus confirms that the primary function of the pyramids was sepulchral. The Egyptian kings, combining in their persons the functions of priest, king and god, strove through all their earthly lives to provide themselves with costly tombs to ensure their survival in the after-life.

Herodotus briefly mentions the extended period of construction of the Great Pyramid and states that it was the tomb of King Cheops. According to the historian, it was erected on the king's orders during his lifetime out of despotic vanity, and a wish to perpetuate his memory for ever.

Four centuries after Herodotus, the great historian and geographer Diodorus Siculus visited the pyramids and left us an account: 'The largest', writes Diodorus, 'is quadrangular, each side at its base is seven hundred feet long, and more than six hundred high; it gradually contracts to the top, where each side is six cubits; it is built entirely of solid stone, of a difficult workmanship, but external duration; for in the thousand years said to have elapsed since their construction, which some make more than three thousand four hundred, the stones have not moved from their original position, but the whole remains uninjured.'

The vast bulk and impressive geometry of the pyramids made them appear in the works of many ancient chroniclers and commentators. The Greek geographer Strabo (c. 63-25 B.C.) visited them, and the Roman soldier-scientist Pliny, in addition to writing on the pyramids, mentioned other authors who had written about them: Euhemerus, Aristagoras, Duris of Samos, Antisthenes (the negativist philosopher), Demetrius, Demoteles and Apion. All their works on the pyramids are now lost, which reminds us of just how fragmentary our written sources of history actually are.

Ancient Egyptian Sacred Geometry

Our interest is, however, in the principles of sacred geometry which underlie the structure of this, and other, pyramids. The Great Pyramid can be seen as the apex of a tradition which began wit h the Step Pyramid of Kin Zoser at Saqqara (c. 2750 B.C.). Several smaller pyramids p re- ate the Great Pyramid, and their designs show an evolutionary pattern which culminated in the Great Pyramid itself. Afterwards, the tradition declined, and a series of degenerate pyramids were constructed, most of which have now disintegrated owing to poor workmanship.

The first true pyramid, the tomb of King Zoser at Saqqara, was designed by Imhotep, a man of exceptional genius - so much so that after his death he was elevated to the status of the god who founded medicine and architecture. The Step Pyramid was of a square ground-plan, and, like the Babylonian ziggurats, was a stepped 'holy mountain' rather than a flush-sided pyramid. It was enclosed in a vast sanctuary in the form of a double square surrounded by a thirty-foot wall. The sanctuary, a massive undertaking in itself, was 1788 feet in length - one third of a mile - and oriented north-south. The form of this enclosure set the pattern for later holy places. It was used, inter alia, centuries later, in the Tabernacle and Temple of the Jews, and as the underlying pattern for the Chapel Royal at Whitehall in London.

The Step Pyramid represents a sudden application of methods which appear to have been formerly unknown. The technology of stone cutting and transport was known, but never before had such a vast undertaking been attempted. In the court of the Step Pyramid stood a statue upon whose plinth was the name Imhotep with the citation 'Chancellor of the King of Lower Egypt, First after the King of Upper Egypt, Administrator of the Great Palace, hereditary nobleman, High Priest of Heliopolis, Builder, Sculptor, and Maker of Vases in Chief'. Such an impressive list of official positions emphasises the exceptional talent of this man, who above all others stands at the head of the Western Tradition of sacred geometry.

Imhotep was the son of Ka-nefer, Director of Works of Upper and Lower Egypt, not a man of royal blood. However, the list of titles from his effigy, and the attributes given to him after his elevation to the pantheon, demonstrate the essential unity of ancient Egyptian magic, religion and technology. The discovery of the tomb of such a seminal figure has long been the cherished dream of Egyptologists. It is believed to be somewhere in the vicinity of Saqqara, but as yet the resting-place of the originator of architecture in the West remains undefiled.

After Zoser's pyramid, another was commenced at Saqqara for King Sekhemket. For some unknown reason, this was abandoned at a height of only twenty feet, and a third step pyramid, at Zawiyet el Aryan, believed to be intended for King Khaba, was also abandoned during construction. After these step pyramids, true pyramids clad in polished fitted casings of Tura limestone were erected.

The first of the true pyramids, that of King Sneferu at Meidum, was a disaster. In his book *The Riddle of the Pyramids*, Kurt Mendelssohn has shown from the configuration of the rubble which surrounds the core of this ruined pyramid that it collapsed during construction. Faulty workmanship, and the innovative nature of the project, caused a sudden collapse. Such a disaster, in a period when scarcely any buildings of any size existed anywhere in the world, must have had a profound effect on the people of the time, and may be enshrined in garbled form in the myth of the Tower of Babel. Like Zoser's pyramid, the Meidum example was designed as a step pyramid, but was filled in with packing blocks and casing. The few remaining casing blocks, excavated from the chaotic pile of rubble which surrounds this pyramid, show that the angle of elevation was 52^0, an angle of great importance in sacred geometry.

When the pyramid at Meidum was overtaken by disaster, another pyramid, at Dahshur, was already under construction. Of all the surviving pyramids, this one is unique. The lower part of the casing rises at an elevation of $54°$, then, at a point about halfway up, it abruptly changes its angle to $43° 30'$. It is probable that the architect of this pyramid altered the angle in order that the disaster of Meidum should not also overtake his building.

However, it is obvious from all the other pyramids that the 'Bent Pyramid', as it is known, was an aberration from an ideal norm. Cased pyramids represent the celestial spectacle of the sun's rays breaking through the clouds after a rainstorm - a manifestation of the divine power of Ra. The changeover from the Imhotep-inspired step pyramids to the pure form appears to have occurred at the same time as the arrival of the priests of Heliopolis in a position of power in Egypt. Most interestingly, their ascendance brought in a new interpretation of sacred geometry: the true pyramid, the obelisk and the ben-ben, the sacred conical pillar of the Temple of Ra at Heliopolis.

After the fiasco of the Bent Pyramid, the next pyramid, which stands a mile to the north of it, was built at the lower angle of $43° 30'$, the angle of the upper half of its predecessor. However, all was not lost. The lessons of these three failures were analyzed, and the construction of the largest structure ever erected by man was commenced: the incomparable Great Pyramid.

The Great Pyramid, ostensibly constructed to house the mortal remains of King Khufu (alternatively known by his Grecian name of Cheops), is built with an all but perfect square ground plan of 755 feet, and an angle of ascent of $51° 52'$. Its bulk is a staggering 621 million tons of limestone. The angle of ascent gives the pyramid a unique geometrical property which represents the mystic squaring of the circle: its height stands in the same ratio to its circumference as does the radius to the circumference of a circle. This ratio is 0.5π =3.1416..., and in this pyramid, this transcendental number is represented with an accuracy of better than 0.1% error.

51^0 52' has the property of being the angle produced by a gradient of 4:1. The angle used at Dahshur, 43^0 30', is produced by a gradient of 3:1. Thus, the simple use of whole numbers, which is the keynote of sacred geometry throughout history, exists in the Egyptian context. 'The existence of the pyramids', wrote James Stirling, in The Canon, '... seems to be a striking confirmation of the statements of the earliest writers, that architecture originally depended on geometry, and we see in Egypt the first application of that science to building ... In the hands of geometrical architects, the pyramid by its bulk, surface, lines and angles, would afford the means of recording measures and numbers. For practical purposes, also, the pyramid is a most suitable form for a permanent fabric.'

Another geometrical characteristic of the pyramids which has been commented upon concerns the faces. The theory has been put forward that the pyramids were conceived as representations of the northern hemisphere on a square projection. Each flat face of the pyramid was designed to represent one curved quadrant of this hemisphere, according to this theory. The pyramid fulfils this geometric consideration like no other figure: to project a spherical quadrant onto a flat triangle, the base of the quadrant must be the same as the base of the triangle, and must also have the same height. This is fulfilled in the Great Pyramid, where the angle of slope gives the ~ relationship between height and base.

The complexities of geometry inherent in the Great Pyramid have been largely unravelled in a plethora of calculation and

Ancient Egyptian Sacred Geometry

theory over the last century or so. Herodotus was told by the Temple priests that the Great Pyramid was constructed in such a way that the area of each face was equal to the square of its height. This relationship can be seen to embody the Golden Section, which according to the modern geometrician Schwaller de Lubicz was seen not in numerical terms but as emblematical of the creative or generative function, the fundamental of an infinite series.

Inside the Great Pyramid is an enigmatic series of passages whose purpose is as yet largely undetermined. These comprise three chambers: the King's Chamber, which contains nothing but an empty sarcophagus; the Queen's Chamber, which is smaller and also empty; and an unfinished chamber in the living rock below ground level. In addition to these three chambers, there is an impressive passage known as the Grand Gallery, lined with carefully-fitted granite casing, and possessing a high corbelled ceiling. However, nothing of note has ever been discovered in the Great Pyramid - a feature which has given the pyramidologists ammunition for their storehouses and observatory theories.

The Danish architect Hubert Paulsen, puzzled by the lack of any contents, claimed that there must be another, as yet undiscovered, chamber within the Great Pyramid. By geometry, he calculated that the true burial chamber, crammed with wealth which would dim the treasures of Tutankhamun - by comparison with Khufu a poor monarch - should be beneath the centre of the pyramid, and below ground level. The King's Chamber, which one would imagine to have been intended for the after-life requisites of the Pharaoh, in addition to being 130 feet above ground level, is not directly beneath the apex of the pyramid. Paulsen's chamber has, unfortunately, not been located, and experiments carried out in Khafre's (Chephren's) Pyramid have also met with failure.

Sacred Geometry

By comparison with the Great Pyramid, whose chambers and passages were revealed by the accidental fall of a ceiling block in the entrance passage, the Pyramid of Khafre is seemingly devoid of passages. One small chamber exists, in the rock beneath the vast bulk of the structure. This has always seemed anomalous to Egyptologists, and an attempt to X-ray' the pyramid was made in 1970 by Professor Luis Alvarez of the University of California. Alvarez attempted to record the passage through the pyramid of cosmic rays, which impinge upon the Earth from outer space. Using extremely sophisticated detection equipment, he made observations over a period of several days. On analysing the results, they showed inexplicable variations which made the experiment inconclusive. The variability of the results were perhaps caused by the geometry of the pyramid, its positioning, its relationship to the Earth's magnetic field, or some combination of these and other factors. Whatever the cause, Alvarez's experiment failed to discern any inner chamber or passages.

Many extravagant claims have been forwarded to interpret the complex array of passages and other internal features of Khufu's pyramid, but in reality none of them seem to deserve any more attention than any other. Of especial note are those theories that the Second Coming of Christ, the end of the world, or some other momentous happening are foretold by various steps, stone joints, passage bends and cracks. Books of pyramid prophecy have an unfortunate propensity of requiring drastic revision when the prophesied apocalypse does not arrive on time. I leave it to the reader to judge the validity of the work of Piazzi Smyth, John Taylor, John Davidson, Edgar Stewart, Basil Steward and their imitators.

Although the pyramids are the most august manifestation of the sacred geometry of Egypt, their geometrically-inspired canonical arts infused all sacred artifacts. Imbotep's title of 'Maker of Vases in Chief' demonstrates that a major geometer was required for the correct design and manufacture of sacred vessels. Products of Egyptian art of whatever period are, with few exceptions, instantly recognisable as such. The style continued for over 3000 years, even into the Hellenic period after Alexander the Great conquered the country. The canonical measures and proportional system, laid down as expressions of a magical view of the world, inhibited any innovation. The role of the artist was thus quite unlike that of his modern counterpart. The concept of the artist as an individual creative personality is absolutely modern. Like other artisans, the majority of sculptors and painters were part of a team which adhered rigidly to the pre-ordained canons of art. Their position can be compared with that of modern designers of printed circuitry or microprocessors, who are constrained within a technological framework of function which depends absolutely upon the laws of electronics.

Like their modern technologist counterparts, the artisans of ancient Egypt were precision workers, early practitioners of the universal belief that acts of magic must be performed according to precise, unchanging ritual. Underlying these ritual forms was geometry.

The technical basis of Egyptian geometry was impeccable. Indeed, the later success of the ancient Greeks, with whom geometry is nowadays most readily associated, was based solidly upon the knowledge and technique of the ancient Egyptians. The practices of Egyptian geometry are not lost, however, as the vast burgeoning of interest in the antiquities of Egypt during the last century led to the rediscovery of its fundamentalist. During his destructive excavations within the fabric of the Great Pyramid, Colonel Howard Vyse found in one of the chambers 'many quarry-marks similar to those in other chambers and also several red lines crossing each other at right angles, with black equilateral triangles, described near the "intersection" in order probably to obtain a right angle ...' These lines and constructions were necessary for the

Sacred Geometry

masonic arts of stone cutting, fitting and finishing. For any technical method of drawing, it is necessary to have a geometrical basis. The use of intersecting lines to mark out the background for a relief carving was systematised into a

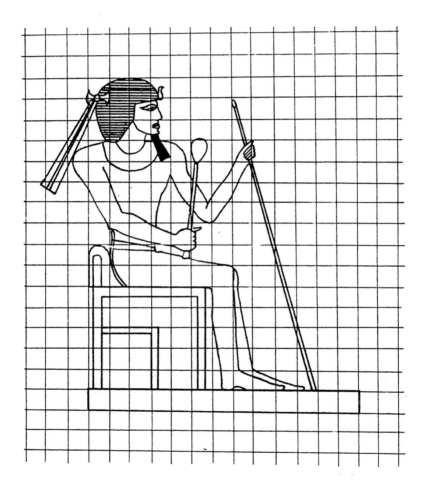

15. An ancient Egyptian canonical master-drawing with a square grid determining the placement of all parts of the image.

square grid. This was an aid not only to the general composition and layout of the work, but also served to ensure that the human figures to be made should be correctly proportioned in accordance with the canon.

Guide lines were painted with a brush or made with a string dipped in red paint, and the outlines were sketched with a brush made of wood fibres or a rush pen such as those used by scribes. The sculptor chiselled around the finalised outlines, and the sculpture was then finished by being covered with a wash of plaster. Finally, it was painted in canonical colours. Root rectangles were used to determine the main dimensions of the figures within a framework which was usually square. Thus dynamic symmetry was canonically infused in the sculpture which reproduced in its dimensions all the sacred attributes of the geometry. This was additional to its figurative and symbolic content. Such rectangles were easily constructed by simple geometry from the square grid which itself had the symbolic meaning of the world, within which the human was the Temple. The fundamental geometry of Temple foundation was reproduced microcosmically in each canonical carving, in accordance with the age-old Temple-body formula, a feature which we can trace throughout the recorded history of architecture.

Such a combination of underlying grid, overlying geometry and outward form gives us a three-layered concept of sacred art without which the multiple forms can scarcely be understood. Such a three-in-one concept, encapsulated in the Trinity of Isis, Horus and Osiris, occurs throughout canonical art from Egypt onwards. In some sacred art the geometrical form is predominant, such as in Celtic interlace work or Islamic tile patterns. This is the second level being manifest. In general this overt form is suppressed. Such geometry has the inherent characteristic of incorporating within itself the sacred metrology of whatever system it represents.

One characteristic of sacred geometry which recurs

throughout time is the choice of geometries which are as inclusive as practically possible. A geometry which includes the square, the circle, the vesica and the equilateral triangle as well as various root rectangles and the Golden Section has been seen as the ideal microcosm. The tomb of King Rameses IV of Egypt is just such an example. Rameses IV was buried in a rock-cut tomb, not a pyramid, as pyramid building had been

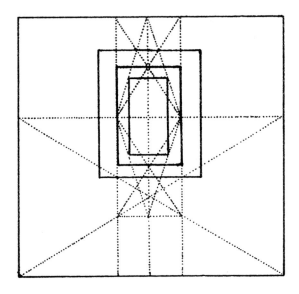

16. Geometric analysis of the tomb of Rameses IV of Egypt - double square and golden section rectangles.

abandoned by his time. The rock-cut tomb contained a triple sarcophagus. The innermost sarcophagus was in the form of a double square, the holiest of sacred enclosures. Surrounding this, the middle sarcophagus had the dimensions of a Golden Section rectangle, and the outer sarcophagus two Golden Section rectangles equal to the middle one. The tomb itself was dimensioned on a projection of the geometry of this triple sarcophagus. Such harmonic geometry, brought to a finely-honed pitch of perfection by the ancient Greeks, was applied throughout Egyptian sacred art. The pectorals and other magic amulets found on mummified Egyptians have been geometrically analyzed. They show this double square- Golden Section geometry, which demonstrates the unity of Egyptian sacred geometry from the largest to the smallest sacred object.

5. Mesopotamian and Hebrew Sacred Geometry

Although the Biblical tale of the fall of the Tower of Babel was probably a garbled folk memory of the collapse during construction of the Meidum Pyramid, the tradition of building artificial holy mountains surmounted by temples is undoubtedly Babylonian. Whatever the origin of the legendary collapse, there was certainly a ziggurat at Babylon whose dimensions and geometry have been reconstructed from documentary and archaeological evidence.

Designed as miniature reproductions of the arrangement of the universe, these holy mountains were oriented foursquare to the cardinal directions. The name given them, ziggurat, signified 'peaks of the gods'. Those excavated in the Mesopotamian cities of Ur, Uruk and Babylon have been estimated to have stood three hundred feet from base to apex. The dimensions of that at Khorsabad were 150 feet square at the base and 135 feet high from the pavement to the platform at its summit.

The structure was comprised of seven stages, each stage representing the attributes of one of the planets and being painted in one of the planetary colours. The ziggurat of Nabu at Borsippa (Barsipki) was known as the 'House of the Seven Bonds of Heaven and Earth' and represented the cosmic link between the earthly and the heavenly planes. James Fergusson, in *A History of Architecture in All Countries* (1893) wrote:

> This temple, as we know from the decipherment of the cylinders which were found on its angles, was dedicated to the seven planets or heavenly spheres, and we find it consequently adorned with the colours of each. The lower, which was also richly panelled, was black, the colour of Saturn; the next, orange, the colour of Jupiter; the third red, emblematic of Mars; the fourth yellow, belonging to the sun; the fifth and sixth green and blue respectively, as dedicated to Venus and Mercury; and the upper probably white, that being the colour belonging to the Moon, whose place in the Chaldean system would be uppermost.

The cosmological link has been worked out by Professor Stecchini, who believes that the seven-stepped ziggurat was a representation of the northern hemisphere of the Earth, the ground level representing the equator, and the apex the pole. In Greek geography, the area between the equator and the pole was divided into seven zones, each smaller than the previous to compensate for the diminishing degree of longitude as one approaches the pole. Stecchini s contention that the ziggurat was representative of the hemisphere is given credence by cuneiform tablets which assert that each level of the ziggurat had a specific area determined by standard units of land measure.

The cuneiform tablet known as the Smith Tablet specifically states that each terrace of the ziggurat of Babylon had its own symbolic measure. This enabled various geometrical schemata to be incorporated into the building. The third step was particularly important because it was in the form of a square with sides of sixty cubits - a fundamental unit of Babylonian land measure. The angle of slope at various points gives important geometrical ratios, such as $\sqrt{5} - 1$, angles fundamental in land surveying, and also found in the Great

Pyramid.

The Boston metrologist Herman Gaylord Wood analyzed cuneiform writing as part of his great survey of ancient metrology and symbolism. He showed that the characters of this writing were derived from the duodecimal division of the circle, and indeed that division is still in use with us today in the clock and the compass.

The influence of Egyptian geometry and Chaldean magic was strongly felt by the Israelites. Throughout the Bible, sacred objects and buildings are described in detail with precise measurements which were believed to have been given by God. The earliest of such canonically dimensioned constructions is the mythological Noah's Ark, which is described as follows:

> Make thee an ark of gopher wood; rooms shalt thou make in the ark, and shalt pitch it within and without with pitch. And this is the fashion which thou shalt make it of; the length of the ark shall be three hundred cubits, the breadth of it fifty cubits, and the height of it thirty cubits. A window shalt thou make to the ark, and in a cubit shalt thou finish it above; and the door of the ark shalt thou set in the side thereof; with lower, second and third storey shalt thou make it.
>
> Genesis 7:1-16.

In Qabalistic tradition, Noah's Ark is divided into three storeys, each with 11 sections, which makes in all the sacred number 33. The Ark has two openings: the main door in the lowest storey through which animal lives pass into the plane of physical existence, and a small one-cubit window at the crown of the head through which the spirit, symbolised by the dove, is liberated.

Several practitioners of occult knowledge have commented on this sacred vessel. Philo Judaeus asserts that the Ark of Noah was constructed after the pattern of the human body. Heinrich Cornelius Agrippa concurs. He writes:

> Seeing man is the most beautiful and perfect work of God, and His image, and also the lesser world; therefore he by a more perfect composition, and sweet harmony, and more sublime dignity doth contain, and maintain in himself all numbers, measures, weights, motions, elements, and all other things, which are of his composition; and in him, as it were, is the supreme workmanship ... moreover God Himself taught Noah to build the Ark according to the measure of a man's body, and He made the whole fabric of the World proportionable to man's body. Therefore some who have written of the microcosm, or of man, measure the body by 6 feet, a foot by 10 degrees, every degree by 5 minutes; from hence are numbered 60 degrees, which make 300 minutes, to the which are compared so many geometrical cubits by which Moses describes the Ark; for as the body of a man is in length 300 minutes, in breadth 50 and in height 30; so the Ark was 300 cubits long, 50 broad and 30 high.

In *The Canon*, William Stirling connects the measures of the Ark with the size of the planet Earth, and the canons of chronology in Hebrew sacred history. 'If this explanation be correct', writes Stirling, 'we must conceive, by the proportions of the ark, the vast figure of a man, in the likeness and the image of God, whose body contains the measure of the sun's path in the ecliptic, the circuit of the Earth, and the orbits of the seven planets.'

Such cosmological schemata can be found throughout ancient architecture, especially in Egypt and Babylonia. The Ark, whilst ostensibly a ship in which one righteous man, his family and livestock escaped an earth wide deluge, in reality is a cosmic image of man the microcosm being fitted anew into

Sacred Geometry

the God-given pattern. Those who fit the cosmic scheme survive, those who do not, perish.

Another Hebrew sacred structure whose dimensions and hence geometry, were precisely delineated was the Tabernacle. This was a portable shrine used by the Jewish people during their wanderings in Sinai. Basically a movable temple, patterned on Egyptian prototypes, the Tabernacle stood inside a court whose geometry was that of the double square, 100 cubits long by 50 cubits wide. This court was demarcated by a fence composed of posts 5 cubits in height set in the ground at intervals of 5 cubits. The posts were connected by strands of twined linen. The whole ground plan of the Tabernacle was thus constructed according to a modular square grid of 5 cubits - the method of layout used in Egypt, from whence the Israelites had just fled.

Inside the double square enclosure, the Tabernacle itself was a triple square 30 cubits long and 10 cubits wide. Its walls were constructed of wooden planks 1.5 cubits wide and 10 cubits high, held in line by strong horizontal bars of wood. The whole structure was covered with skins sewn together in strips 30 cubits long by 4 cubits wide. The Tabernacle was placed in the court towards the west, but with its entrance oriented eastwards, so that, according to Josephus 'when the sun arose it might send its first rays upon it.

Such an orientation, which is common in sacred architecture throughout the world, ensures that the fabric of the shrine is directly integrated with cosmic phenomena. This is of fundamental importance at the astronomically-defined times for the performance of vital rituals. As a microcosm, it was necessary that the temple or Tabernacle should directly reflect in its dimensions, geometry and orientation the conditions and structure of the macrocosm of which it was at once an image and a means of direct access. Indeed, Josephus asserts that 'this proportion of the measures of the Tabernacle proved to be an imitation of the system of the world.'

The interior of the Tabernacle was divided into two compartments, a scheme which was to be copied later in the Temple built at Jerusalem on the orders of King Solomon. The outer compartment, called the Holy Place, was a double square 20 by 10 cubits, whilst the inner compartment, the Holy of Holies, comprised a single square. As the height of the Tabernacle's ceiling was also 10 cubits, the Holy of Holies enclosure was thus a perfect cube.

Inside the Holy of Holies was the most sacred object of the Jews, the Ark of the Covenant. Like other Jewish sacred objects, its precise measures are recorded. In length the Ark measured 2.5 cubits, half the module used in the layout of the Tabernacle, and in breadth and height it was 1.5 cubits. Stirling believed that these measures had cosmological significance:

> It measured 2.5 cubits long, or 3.25 feet, or 45 inches; its breadth and height were 1.5 cubits, or 2.5 feet, or 27 inches. Its perimeter was therefore the mystic number of 144 inches. If the Ark were rather more than an inch thick, which would be sufficient for a box of this size, its contents would amount to 24,860 cubic inches, or the number of miles in the circumference of the Earth.

This fascinating interpretation, of course, hinges upon the antiquity of the inch and mile, a knotty problem made no easier by the extravagant claims which have been advanced in interpretation of the mysteries of the Great Pyramid.

Another geometrically-determined object kept in the Tabernacle was the Table of Shewbread, modelled on an Egyptian prototype. This sacred table stood outside of the veil which divided the Tabernacle, and was thus not in the Holy of Holies itself. Its dimensions were 2.5 cubits by 1.5 cubits by 1

Sacred Geometry

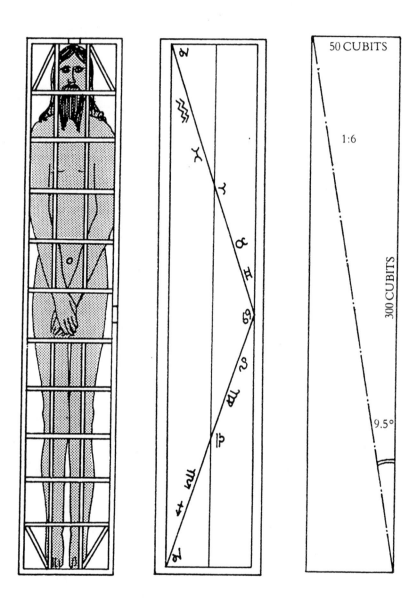

17. Noah's Ark, symbolic of God's creation and the zodiacal year.

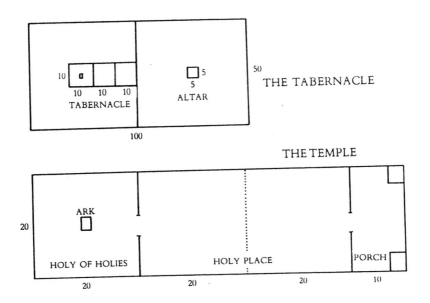

18. The tabernacle of the Jews. Double Square. The Temple of Solomon at Jerusalem, triple square.

cubit. a ratio of 5:3:2.

The Altar of Sacrifice was the outer equivalent of the Ark of the Covenant. It stood at the centre of the outer of the two squares of the enclosure. The base of this altar was a square 5 X 5 cubits, the layout module. This altar represented one of the two poles at the centre of the two squares - each upon its own centre of polarity - the combination of the two within the court of the Tabernacle being the unity of opposites inherent in the supreme God. Such a precise dimensioning and laying-out of a sacred area affords us with a rare glimpse of sacred geometry at its most canonical. Each and every object is precisely and accurately defined in size and location, for to alter anything would be to court disaster.

Sacred Geometry

The national life of the Jews reached its climax during the reign of King Solomon. In 1004 B.C., the crowning act of his reign was the erection of a temple to the worship of Jahweh. Like other Hebrew sacred artifacts, the design of the Temple had been divinely revealed, to Solomon's father, King David:

> Then David gave to Solomon his son the pattern of the porch, and of the houses thereof, and of the upper chambers thereof, and of the inner parlour thereof, and of the place of the mercy seat. And the pattern of all that he had by the spirit, and the courts of the house of the Lord ...
> I Chronicles 28

The dimensions of the Temple, like the Tabernacle before it, were precisely detailed:

> Now these are the things wherein Solomon was instructed for the building of the House of God. The length by cubits after the first measure was threescore cubits, and the breadth twenty cubits.
> II Chronicles 3

A triple square double the size of the Tabernacle, the walls of the Temple were hewn stone lined inside with wood overlaid with gold. The interior comprised a double-square rectangular holy place, and a single-square Holy of Holies. The interior was 20 cubits high, making the Holy of Holies again a cubic enclosure.

At the very centre of the Holy of Holies stood the Ark of the Covenant, which formerly had occupied the central point of the Holy of Holies of the Tabernacle. At each end of the Ark was a golden cherub with wings outstretched, ten cubits in height. This ten cubits appears to have been the module from which the dimensions of the Temple derived and was double the size of the portable Tabernacle.

The entrance to the Holy of Holies was closed by a two-leaved door, each leaf two cubits in width. The actual entrance to the Temple was 5 cubits in width, and opened from a porch which comprised two squares of 10 x 10 cubits. It was this porch which supported the two pillars which subsequently became of utmost significance in Masonic lore: Jachin and Boaz.

Each pillar was 12 cubits in circumference and was surmounted by a lily-shaped capital 5 cubits in height. This rested on a pommel 3 cubits high which bore 7 chains of pomegranates, 14 in all. This mystic number 14 corresponds with the 14 squares of 10 cubits comprising the ground plan of the Temple; St Matthew's traditional 14 generations from Abraham to David; and the 14 Christian Stations of the Cross. Again, the Temple incorporated various cosmological schemata as befitting an image of the macrocosmos. This first Temple of Jerusalem, the Temple of Solomon, was destroyed in 585 B.C. when the Babylonians took the city and deported the larger proportion of the populace as slaves. When the long captivity of the Jews in Babylon finally ended, the returning captives found the Temple razed to the ground. The Book of Esdras gives the following account:

> In the first year that King Cyrus reigned over the country of Babylon Cyrus the King wrote to build up this house. And the holy vessels of gold and silver, that Nabuchodonosor had carried away out of the house at Jerusalem ... those Cyrus the king brought forth out of the temple at Babylon, and they were delivered to Zorobabel and to Sanabassarus the ruler ... then the same Sanabassarus, being come hither, laid the foundations of the house of the Lord at Jerusalem ... in the first year of Cyrus, King Cyrus commanded that the house of the Lord at Jerusalem should be built again, where they do sacrifice with continual fire. Whose height shall be sixty cubits, and the breadth sixty cubits, with

three rows of hewn stones, and one row of new wood of that country...

Thus the second temple, built on the express orders of the Persian conqueror, was a square structure with sides of 60 cubits. Height is an old term sometimes used to mean length, but it is possible that the temple may have been in the form of a ziggurat. If this is so, it would have been of four stages ('rows' of hewn stone and wood). Whichever form the temple took, its dimensions were based upon the old temple, as 60 cubits was its length excluding the porch of Boaz and jachin.

Little else is recorded concerning this temple, except that all of the holy objects which had been carried off to Babylon and installed in the chief temple there were returned and again used in Jewish observances. The form of the second temple, a square, was uncharacteristic for the Jews, and must have been of Persian origin. According to the Talmud, the first temple was constructed by supernatural means, and according to the Bible by Phoenician workmen under the direction of Hiram Abiff. If the second temple was of Persian workmanship, its variation in design may be accounted for by the rapidity of its erection - during the first year of liberation. However, like the first temple, it was destined to be razed by invaders.

In the First Book of Maccabees it is recorded that 'when they saw the sanctuary desolate, and the altar profaned and the gates burned up, and shrubs growing in the courts as in a forest ... they rent their clothes and made great lamentation, and cast ashes upon their heads.' However, the techniques and knowledge involved in the reconstruction of the Temple had been lost, and instead of rebuilding it, Judas Maccabeus and his men pulled down the remains. 'They thought it best to pull it down, lest it should be a reproach to them, because the heathen had defiled it: wherefore they pulled it down. And laid up the stones in the mountain of the temple in a

Mesopotamian and Hebrew Sacred Geometry

convenient place, until there should come a prophet to show what should be done with them.'

This shows that the knowledge of sacred geometry required to erect a new holy edifice was lacking from the pious but profane and military band of Judas. A prophet with the appropriate esoteric knowledge was required, but was lacking. A replacement temple was not constructed until the era of Herod, who built an exact replica of Solomon's shrine. Only a single wall of Herod's Temple now survives, in the shape of the famous 'Wailing Wall'. The temple itself was razed yet again, this time by the Romans in their colonial war against the Jews in the year A.D. 70.

6. Ancient Greece

> From harmony, from heavenly harmony
>   This universal frame began;
>   From harmony to harmony
> Thro' all the compass of the notes it ran,
>   The diapason closing full in man.
>
> Dryden: A Song for St Cecilia's Day.

The ancient Greeks were noted for their pioneering and experimental approach towards the world. Numerous philosophers set up theories which others disputed with reasoned argument and practical experiment. In this heady milieu, an important discovery which had a great bearing on sacred geometry was made by Pythagoras in the late sixth century B.C. He discovered that tuned strings on a musical instrument sound in harmony when their lengths are related to each other by certain whole numbers.

Pythagoras had made the radically important discovery that tones can be measured in terms of space. He found that musical consonances can be expressed in ratios of whole numbers. For instance, if two strings vibrate under the same conditions, one being half the length of the other, the pitch of the shorter string will be a diapason (octave) above the longer. If the strings have a length ratio of 2:3, the pitch difference will be a diapente (fifth), and if the length ratio is 3:4, the difference will be a diatessaron (fourth). These Pythagorean consonances are thus expressed in terms of simple progression 1:2:3:4, which contains in addition to diapason, diatessaron and diapente, octave-and-a-fifth, 1:2:3; and two octaves, 1:2:4.

When this scheme was re-publicised in the sixteenth century of the Christian Era, it formed the basis of the harmonic systems of Renaissance sacred architecture. Pythagoras's discovery was seen in terms of a divine revelation of the universal harmony. The whole universe could now be explained in mathematical terms. In order to achieve mastery of this universe, the Pythagoreans claimed, man had to discover the numbers hidden in all things. The revival of this doctrine twenty-two centuries later was responsible for the explosive development of science which has re-shaped the world into its modern image.

The Pythagoreans held that numbers were independent units which possessed certain indivisible and eternal spatial dimensions. However, despite this theory, they were practical enough to realise that, for instance, the diagonals of squares are not measurable in whole units. Pythagoras called such numbers measureless'. Later, such numbers as $\sqrt{3}$ were to be dubbed irrational', i.e., inexpressible in measure. As it was, the Pythagorean idea of finite units was rapidly criticised by Zeno, who, by means of his famous paradox, discredited the theory.

Pythagoras claimed that these numbers and their proportions were fundamental to the fabric of the whole world. The cube was the culminating perfection, for it is impossible in classical geometry to proceed further than the third dimension of length, width and height. Following on Pythagorean number lore, Plato (428-347 B.C.) in his Timaeus asserted that the cosmic harmony is contained in certain numbers formed in the cubes and squares of the double and triple proportion

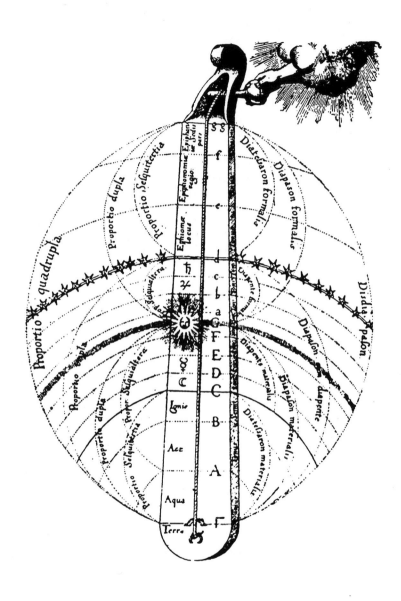

19. The Divine Harmony. The planets and the elements related to the proportion of the cosmic continuum. From Fludd.

Ancient Greece

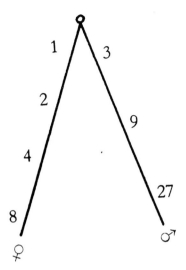

20. The Lambda.

commencing at unity. These are created by the two geometrical progressions 1, 2, 4, 8 and 1, 3, 9, 27. Traditionally represented in the form of the Greek letter lambda λ, they pervade the European geometric tradition from Greece to the modern era. To Plato, the harmony of the universe was expressed in seven numbers (seven is itself a mystical number): 1, 2, 3, 4, 8, 9, 27, figures which encompass the mysteries of macrocosm and microcosm, numbers suited above all others for incorporation in sacred architecture.

In his prescription for the foundation of a new city, Plato stated that all details required the closest attention. He asserted that the temples ought to be arranged around a marketplace and throughout the city on high points. The geometrical nature of the city's plan was taken for granted. Its geomantic design was to be regulated by an Urban Commission with powers to prohibit any unauthorised alterations to the overall scheme. This geomantic design which governed the city was held to be essential for the happiness of the inhabitants. Plato believed that people would never know happiness until the designers of their cities were artists who took the divine as their pattern.

This divine pattern, as enumerated in Plato's *Republic*, was a cosmological scheme representing the microcosm. Even the number of inhabitants of the city was ideal - 5040 landholders occupying the same number of plots. This number is almost universally divisible, being derived from the successive multiplication of the numbers 1 to 7, and hence is divisible by all the numbers from 1 to 10 as well as 12. The whole country surrounding the acropolis was to be divided into 12 parts, but equality was to be ensured by the ingenious provision that allotments of bad land should be larger than allotments of good land, a difficult, if not impossible, task. The *Republic* was an allegorical microcosm in every sense. Its geometrical and numerological attributes all reflect the divine ideal, the consummation of which, if achieved, would render man at one with the universe - the final goal of magicians and alchemists throughout time.

The most famous geometer of all time, Euclid, was, of course, Greek. His work, known as the *Elements*, became the standard textbook of geometry until the present century. In it, through many theorems and proofs, the basic relationships of geometry were defined in a rational manner. His geometry was purely theoretical, and may represent the first time in history that theory was studied for its own sake and not as an integral part of praxis. In Euclid, practical geometry is directly related to whole number ratios which eliminate any necessity to measure angles. Thus, until the Renaissance, when number and angular measurement became important with the use of artillery, whole number ratios were invariably employed in sacred architecture.

In his book *A History of Architecture in All Countries*, James Fergusson writes:

> The system of definite proportion which the Greeks employed in the design of their temples, was another cause of the effect they produce even on uneducated minds. It was not with them merely that the height was equal to the width, or the length about twice the breadth; but every part was proportioned to all those parts with which it was related, in some such ratio as 1 to 6, 2 to 7, 3 to 8, 4 to 9, or 5 to 10, etc. As the scheme advances these numbers become undesirably high. In this case they reverted to some such simple ratio as 4 to 5, 5 to 6, 6 to 7 and so on.

This proportion is nowhere as apparent as in the Parthenon in Athens. This magnificent Pagan temple, now ruined, was constructed as a replacement for a smaller temple of Athena which had been destroyed by the Persians in 480 B.C. Because it was built on the foundations of an earlier temple which itself had superseded a Mycenaean Throne Room, the Parthenon was laid out in Mycenaean measure rather than the current Greek foot. The major dimensions were so chosen that they were round figures in both Greek and Mycenaean feet, not a difficult task as the measures are related in the ratio 10:9. Such a simple relationship is often encountered in related measures such as the Welsh, English and Saxon feet.

The geometry of the Parthenon was such that it incorporated significant measures. Its dimensions were meticulously recorded by an English architect, Francis Cranmer Penrose, who measured the temple with a precision to one thousandth of an English foot. Penrose determined that the Parthenon was not laid out with straight lines, but instead utilised subtle mathematical curves in its fabric. Thus the Parthenon represents another order of geometry, something quite out of the ordinary. Penrose determined that there are essential similarities between the geometrical structure of the Parthenon and the Great Pyramid. The elevations of the fronts of the Parthenon were determined by the Golden Section and the sides were based upon the factor π. Professor Stecchini has calculated that the slight deviations found in the bases of both the Parthenon and the Great Pyramid were deliberate and not the result of slight miscalculations. In his view, the ϕ to π relationship of end to side in the Parthenon parallels that of the north face of the Pyramid (ϕ) to the west face (π).

The width of the fronts of the Parthenon were such as to indicate a second of a degree at the equator. Thus, the individual parts of the fabric, all proportioned commensurably with the underlying geometry of the whole edifice, were in turn proportioned with regard to the dimensions of the Earth itself. The divine harmony thus engendered integrates the building with the cosmos. It becomes an integral part of the overall harmony of the world and is thus a perfect vessel for worship. The threefold necessities for a functional temple - orientation, geometry and measure - are found in the Parthenon and every other truly sacred building planted on the Earth. This degree of integration is attainable by no other method.

Geometry pervaded every sphere of Greek life. The intimate connection between geometric form and sacred history there is seen in the supposedly insoluble problem of the duplication of the cube. The Delians, who, in the time of Plato were suffering a pestilence, consulted the oracle for a means of deliverance. The oracle ordered them to double one of their cubic altars. They therefore sent to the geometers of the Academy, begging them to solve the problem as a matter of national urgency. In reality, it is a problem insoluble by the classical methods of geometry and hence is excluded from the category of sacred geometry. It is equivalent in geometric terms with finding the cube root of two and it can neither be expressed in terms of whole numbers nor in terms of square roots of whole numbers. That such a problem was set by the oracle indicates the seriousness with which geometry was invested in ancient Greece. The correct observance of geometrical form in sacred architecture was a magical act which could deliver a country from trouble.

The duplication of the cube was mentioned in a Greek play, now lost. The geographer Eratosthenes, who used his geometrical knowledge to measure the size of the Earth, relates in a letter to King Ptolemy Ill of Egypt that one of the old Tragic poets refers to the problem. In the play, he introduced King Minos on stage erecting a tomb for his son Glaucos, and then, perceiving the structure to be too mean for a royal mausoleum, he said 'double it but preserve the cubical form'.

These two examples emphasize the importance of volume in Egypto-Greek sacred architecture. Like the internal dimensions of the coffer inside the Great Pyramid, the capacity of sacred structures was of primary concern. Later examples from Medieval and Renaissance Europe also show that capacity was the major determining factor. Internal dimensions were always stipulated in the design of churches and chapels, whilst elevational sacred geometry was applied to the exterior elevations. The 'Delian problem', as it is known, of duplicating the cube, was reduced by Hippocrates of Chios to a question of plane geometry, namely, finding the two mean proportionals between two given straight lines, the greater of which is double the lesser. This was but another of the theoretical problems for which Euclid and his followers were known. It led to the discovery of conic sections.

Even at this early period, this literally Academic interest in geometry was dividing the subject into two separate disciplines, the practical and the mathematical. Whilst there was (and still is) a great overlap between sacred and

Sacred Geometry

mathematical geometry, the roots of the schism can be traced to the efforts made by Greek philosophers to solve the geometrical problems of the oracle.

The beauty of Greek art was the practical result of the musings of the philosophers. In those times, when the ancient Pagan reverence for the world had not yet been superseded by the cost-efficient plunder which characterises industrial civilization, every object which passed through the craftsman's hands contained within it sacred properties. The craftsman, unlike his modern counterpart on the production line, was aware of the sacred nature of the materials with which he was working, and his responsibility as trustee of the material he was handling.

Because all the Earth was sacred, the materials were also sacred and thus the moulding of them was an act of worship. It was imperative that the craftsman should perform to the best of his ability and in accordance with the materials at his disposal, and so an application of sacred geometry was perfectly natural. The exquisitely beautiful Greek vases have been analyzed by modern geometricians like Caskey and Hambidge, who found that they were designed according to complex but harmonious constructions of Golden Section geometry. Making vases and sacred utensils according to sacred geometry would ensure their correct function not only in the surroundings of the temple whose geometry they echoed, but also in the secular context. It is only in modern times that sacred geometry has been relegated first to the narrow sphere of the design of sacred buildings and then abolished entirely for all practical purposes.

7. Vitruvius

The necessity of the architect is to create that unison of parts and details which in the best buildings of any time miraculously traced back the imaginative processes to mathematical quantities and geometrical contexts.

Erich Mendelsohn (1887-1953)

Marcus Vitruvius Pollo, commonly known as Vitruvius, was a Roman architect and engineer who worked in the first century before the present era. He was the author of a detailed theoretical and technical treatise which survives as the oldest and most influential work on architecture.

Vitruvius's position as the most influential architect of all time is attested by his following. For centuries, the detailed instructions given in the *Ten Books of Architecture* were more or less faithfully followed throughout the span of time covered by the Roman Empire. After the fall of the Empire, barbarian forms of architecture were introduced, and the canonical instructions of Vitruvius were largely ignored or perverted.

After almost a millennium of obscurity, the rediscovery of his works heralded the renaissance in architecture, when his book suddenly became the chief authority consulted by architects. His precepts were henceforth accepted as sacrosanct. Indeed, the greatest architects of the Renaissance in Italy - Michelangelo, Bramante, Vignola and Palladio - were all ardent students of Vitruvius's work and each and every of their masterpieces derives directly from the proportional systems enumerated in Vitruvius.

The *Ten Books* written by Vitruvius are a full account of architecture, from the initial education of the architect, through the fundamental principles of the art, the geomentic siting of temples and cities, dwelling houses, materials and forms of architecture to painting, machinery and the military arts. According to Vitruvius, architecture depends on order, arrangement, eurhythmy, symmetry, propriety and economy. Order gives due measure to the members of a work considered separately, and symmetrical agreement to the proportions of a whole building. Arrangement involves the placement of things in their proper order, its forms of expression being ground plan, elevation and perspective. It includes the proper successive use of the compasses and rule, the fundamental artifice of the geometer.

Eurythmy is beauty and fitness in the adjustment of the members. Vitruvius asserts that when perfect commodulation (the linking of all the architectural elements with the whole by means of a system of proportion) is achieved, eurythmy is obtained. This was not always possible for technical reasons, but dynamic symmetry, a concept found in the writings of Plato, often proved to be an acceptable substitute. In dynamic symmetry, although the linear elements are not commensurable, the surfaces constructed upon them may be commensurable, linked through rational proportion.

Symmetry is the proper agreement between the parts of the work itself, and the relation between the different elements and the whole general scheme in accordance with a certain part selected as the standard. Thus, in the human body Vitruvius demonstrates the symmetrical harmony which exists between the forearm, foot, palm, finger, and other small parts. These he compares with the parts of a building, continuing the age-old tradition of the sacred edifice seen in terms of the body of man and thus of the microcosm.

Propriety Vitruvius defines as that perfection of style which comes when a work is authoritatively constructed according to canonical principles. Propriety arises from the word prescription, the accepted methods for the construction of the temples of the gods. Vitruvius may be thanked for preserving these prescribed forms: for hypaethral edifices, open to the sky, in honour of jupiter, Lightning, the Heavens, the Sun or the Moon; for Minerva, Mars and Hercules, the Doric Order; for Venus, Proserpine, Flora, Spring-water and the Nymphs, the Corinthian Order; and for Juno, Diana, Bacchus and other gods of that kind, the Ionic Order. Propriety, however, was also deemed to be attainable by the erection of temples in healthy neighbourhoods where suitable springs existed. At these

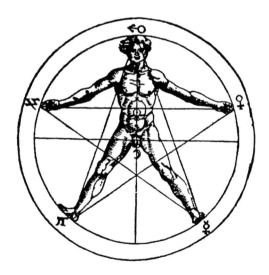

21. Vitruvian Man superimposed on the pentagram. From Fludd.

springs, the shrines were to be built, one of the fundamental principles for temples underlying what is now known as geomancy. Propriety was also gained by the appropriate orientation of buildings so that the light could be utilised to the utmost benefit of all.

Economy, the last Vitruvian tenet, is self-explanatory. All of his maxims echo the down-to-earth functionalism of the ancient world, allowing for all conditions before deciding upon the form of a building whilst under the overall control of sacred geometry. Thus a synthesis of natural and artificial, earthly and heavenly, was arrived at, the balance which the modern ecological movement is striving so hard to regain. Vitruvius, steeped in the ancient geomantic harmony between man and the world, saw the building's design in terms of the body of a man. The well-known designs which show a man's body superimposed on geometry are known to this day as Vitruvian Man. However, not all Vitruvian architecture is related to the proportions of a man's body. This is reserved for temples. The structure of the theatre and the city, constructions with materially different functions, are instead related to the conceptual form of the world and are radial rather than linear.

The construction of the theatre, first put into writing by Vitruvius, but certainly of much greater antiquity, demonstrates its nature as a microcosm of the world. This idea was later to be taken up in the Renaissance and enshrined in Shakespeare's 'All the world's a stage ...', and indeed, physically in this theatre, the aptly-named Globe. Vitruvius's prescribed structure of the theatre was as follows: 'Having fixed upon the principal centre, draw a line of circumference equivalent to what is to be the perimeter at the bottom, and in it inscribe four equilateral triangles, at equal distances apart and touching the boundary of the circle, as the astrologers do in a figure of the twelve signs of the zodiac, when they are making calculations from the musical harmony of the stars.' From this *ad triangulum* layout, the various key parts of the theatre were proportioned. Even the scenery was based upon the triangle, being upon 'triangular pieces of machinery which revolve, each having three decorated faces ... There are three kinds of scenes, one called the tragic, the second the comic and the third the satyric ...' Even the events portrayed in this Roman theatre were divided into three.

However, this was not the only type of theatre described by Vitruvius. The Greek theatre was based upon three squares rather than four triangles, a subtly altered twelvefold geometry which afforded an alternative distribution of the elements in keeping with the different nature of the dramas enacted there.

Vitruvius's pronouncement on Greek symmetry is perhaps the most telling of his expositions of the function of sacred geometry, and its position in the mainstream of Hermetic thought.

> The several parts which constitute a temple ought to be subject to the laws of symmetry; the principles of which should be familiar to all who profess the science of architecture ... Proportion is the commensuration of the various constituent parts with the whole, in the existence of which symmetry is found to consist. For no building can possess the attributes of composition in which symmetry and proportion are disregarded; nor unless there exists the perfect conformation of parts which may be observed in a well formed human being ... therefore, the human frame appears to have been formed with such propriety that the several members are commensurate with the whole.

Vitruvius's work on architecture was an attempt to compile a complete compendium of applied knowledge. To this end, he enunciated not only the sacred geometry of parts of buildings

Sacred Geometry

and their relationship to whole buildings, but also the layout of cities. After describing the attributes for the site of a city, he enumerates the points which the ideal city ought to have. Naturally, his city was based upon a rigorous geometry, but, also being an ideal scheme, was never constructed during the duration of the Roman Empire. One thousand five hundred years were to pass before such a planned city was started.

The Vitruvian City as it is known was planned on an octagonal form. This design runs counter to the standard Roman Colonia then prevalent, which was a quartered rectangle. The octagonal city was divided according to the 'winds'. Vitruvius takes the concept of the eight winds seriously, though he may well have done this in order to conceal a more esoteric doctrine of geometry. Traditionally, the eight directions of the compass were each named after a 'wind'. The system was still in use in Italy as late as the seventeenth century of the present era on surveying instruments. A circumferentor made in Modena in 1686 and now in London's Science Museum, sports a brass dial upon which are engraved the names of the thirty-two winds, a development of those used in Vitruvian days.

In order to divide the circle to determine the directions of the eight winds, Vitruvius uses a classical method of geometry. Like the Hindu Manasara Shilva Shastra, the original omphalos from which the geometry is derived is marked by a gnomon. This central point was marked at Athens by the octagonal Tower of the Winds. Vitruvius gives precise instructions:

> At about the fifth hour of the morning, take the end of the shadow cast by this gnomon, and mark it with a point. Then, opening your compasses to the point which marks the length of the gnomon's shadow, describe a circle from the centre. In the afternoon, watch the shadow of the gnomon as it lengthens, and when it again

touches the circumference of the circle, and the shadow is equal in length to that of the morning, mark it with a point. From these two points describe with your compasses intersecting arcs, and through their intersection and the centre let a line be drawn to the circumference of the circle as a diameter to give the quarters of north and south. Then, using a sixteenth part of the entire circumference of the circle as a diameter, describe a circle ... from the four points thus described draw lines intersecting the centre from one side of the circumference to the other. Thus we shall have an eighth part of the circumference set out for

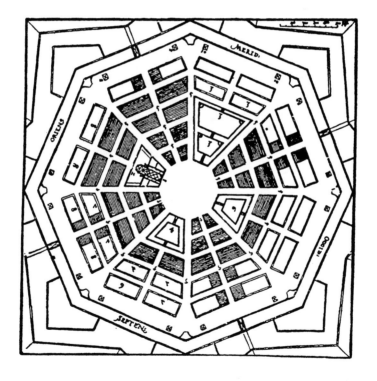

22. Seventeenth-century Vitruvian city plan, showing eightfold division.

Sacred Geometry

Auster and another for Septentrio. The rest of the entire circumference is then to be divided into three equal parts on each side, and thus we have designed a figure equally apportioned among the eight winds.

The geometry here was directly related to the astronomical conditions on the day chosen for the foundation of the city. As that day would have been chosen according to auspicious astrological aspects, the layout was thus related directly to those aspects, reproducing the age-old maxim 'as above, so below Like Plato's *Republic*, the City of Vitruvius was more a cosmic ideal than intended to be a concrete reality on this earth. As in all mystic architecture before the resent century, the symbolic nuministic aspect was held to be the true form whilst the material manifestation was seen as a mere shadow of its spiritual counterpart. Sacred geometry enabled the architect to create a functioning instrument in which the esoteric form's many attributes on the psychological and spiritual levels could be utilised to the utmost. Often, the exigencies of construction made the final result fall short of this ideal, but occasionally every factor was present and a masterpiece ensued. Such masterpieces were to be the models for the Renaissance mystics fifteen hundred years later.

8. The Comacines and Medieval Sacred Geometry

Through good gemetry,
Thys onest craft of good masonry
Was ordeynt and made in thys manere,
Y-cownterfetyd of thys clerkys y-fere;
At these lordys prayers they cownterfetyd gemetry,
And gaf hyt the name of masonry -
Far the most oneste craft of alle.

Ars Gemetrie (fourteenth century)

When the Western Roman Empire collapsed under the onslaught of successive waves of migrating barbarians, the erection of large-scale architectural works came to a halt. There was no longer the politic-economic structure to plan or pay for large civic or ecclesiastical works and hence the widespread skills which formerly existed gradually dwindled. Although Vitruvian knowledge survived intact in the realms of Constantinople, it was all but cut off from the West, which took a different direction.

With barbarian influence, the pure Classical forms of Rome gradually transformed themselves into a radically different architecture - the medieval. The carefully-controlled College of

Architects at Rome was disbanded, and individual ideas and influences were assimilated. With the loss of a central authority, autonomous bands of men with architectural knowledge set themselves up into a sort of federation of journeyman masons - the forerunners of the medieval freemasons who had sole control over the construction of the later cathedrals. According to ancient masonic tradition, refugee members of the disbanded Roman College of Architects fled to Comacina, a fortified island in Italy's Lake Como, where for twenty years they resisted the inroads of the Lombards who were then invading the country. When they were finally overcome, the Lombardic kings took the architects into their employ to aid reconstruction. From this centre, so legend asserts, the masons, who had been dubbed Comacines after their fortified retreat, spread out through western and northern Europe, building churches, castles and civic works for the rulers of the nascent nation states which followed the Roman Empire.

Comacines were certainly in the employ of Rotharis, a Lombard king, who on 22 November 643 issued an edict concerning, among other matters, the Comacines. The title of Article 143 of this edict was *Of the Magistri Comacini and their Colleges*. Article 144 reads: 'If any person has engaged or hired one or more of the Comacine Masters to design a work ... and it should happen that some Comacine should be killed, the owner of the house is not considered responsible.' This seems to infer that the Comacines were a powerful body from which the king felt his subjects needed some protection. Joseph Fort Newton, in his masonic book The Master Builders, tells of an inscribed stone of the year 712 which showed that the Comacine guild was organized in three ranks, discipuli and magistri under a gastaldo, a Grand Master.

Like any group of technicians with sought-after skills, the Comacines were in a position of power and influence. In Northern Europe, where all traces of Roman architectural practice had been stamped out, the Comacine was especially in demand. Like the wizards, soothsayers, astrologers and geomancers who surrounded the court, no respecting Dark Ages king would be without his entourage of Comacines. During his reign, they built his palaces, chapels and churches; on his death, impressive mausolea like Theodoric's at Ravenna in Italy or Aethelbald's at Repton in England. These churches and mausolea were the repository of the Comacines knowledge of sacred geometry.

The venerable Bede, in his *The Lives of the Abbots*, tells us that in the year 674, King Ecgfrith of Northumbria decided to found a monastery for Benedict, his local holy man. To this end, he donated seventy hides of his own estate at Wearmouth (a hide is a unit of land measure of about 120 acres). 'After the space of no more than one year from the monastery's foundation, Benedict crossed the sea and went to Gaul and sought, obtained, and brought back with him masons to build him a church in the Roman style, which he had always loved.'

The stone churches of Northumbria and the masterpieces erected after the renaissance instigated by the Emperor Charlemagne show a gradual increase in complexity and sophistication. A major landmark in this process is the Chapel Palatine at Aachen (Aix-la-Chapelle). A round church, based on the octagram, the chapel shows a return of the influences of the Eastern Empire, which at that time still flourished around Constantinople.

However, contemporary churches in England show a simpler geometrical basis. Analysis of several Saxon Churches in Essex has shown that by a simple method of construction root 3, 4, 5, 6 and even root 7 rectangles were generated for the ground plans. The churches at Inworth, Strethall, Chickney, Hadstock, Little Bardfield, Fobbing, Corringham and White Roding all have length-to-width ratios approximating on root 3. The geometrical proportion, uncommon in later times, was

Sacred Geometry

the result of laying-out foundation trenches with the cord, just like ancient Egyptian practice.

The orientation of the centre-line was laid out by direct observation of sunrise on the patronal day. The master mason would mark off the pre-arranged width of the church to the south of the centreline. An assistant would then walk to the north end of the same line, paying out cord. From this, a square would be made, and from that square, a diagonal taken. The diagonal was then laid out as a length, making a root 2 rectangle. This rectangle's diagonal would then be taken with the cord, and a root 3 rectangle would thus be obtained. The rectangle of the nave s ground-plan could then be completed by using the cord to check the equality of the diagonals.

This method appears to be peculiarly Saxon, as the later Norman churches in the area were generally constructed on the ad quadra turn double square. Charlemagne's masons used the methods later adopted by the Normans, and these 'barbarian' methods of sacred geometry were relegated to the arena of vernacular secular architecture. Charlemagne's architecture, and its imitations, were a conscious revival of the mainstream of Roman methods, being based upon the celebrated round church of San Vitale at Ravenna in Italy. This microcosmic structure, whose purpose was demonstrated to the cognoscenti by a central pavement mosaic in the form of a labyrinth, was built in the sixth century by masons from Constantinople who had absorbed some Asiatic constructional methods and geometry. However, it was not until several centuries later that an influx of Arab ideas was combined with a developed Roman consciousness to create the great cathedrals of the Gothic period.

The infusion of ideas borrowed from the Islamic world marked an important development in the history of Western sacred architecture. The geometrical ideas and practices of the late

Classical world had been taken over by the Arabs when they conquered key university cities like Alexandria several centuries earlier. Texts like Euclid's Elements of Geometry were translated into Arabic and applied to the new sacred architecture demanded by the nascent faith of Islam. Great strides in astronomy, architecture and alchemy had been made by the Arabs, who at one time were several centuries ahead of their European counterparts.

By the eleventh century, however, with the emergence of relatively stable nation states, techniques of building in Europe had reached a high peak of perfection in the Romanesque style, surpassing even the best that the old Roman Empire had to offer. Large arch construction had been mastered, and builders had so perfected mortar joints that a chronicler of the early twelfth century was able to comment that the stones of Old Sarum cathedral, begun in 1102, were so accurately set that the whole work might be thought to be cut out of a single rock.

To this height of perfection a new element was brought - the pointed arch, a geometrical revolution originating in Islamic sacred architecture. The origin of the pointed arch in Europe has been determined as being at the Italian Benedictine monastery of Monte Cassino, built 1066-71. Some, if not all, of the masons who worked on this project were citizens of Amalfi, an Italian commercial republic which had trading stations in places as distant as Baghdad. With this known interchange, it was only a matter of time until all the geometric secrets of the Arab masons were incorporated into Western sacred architecture to form a new transcendent style - now known universally by its eighteenth-century derogatory name, Gothic.

The pointed arch which heralded this revolution is generated by the intersection of two arcs. In its perfect form, this arch is the top half of the vesica piscis. It is a strange coincidence that

Sacred Geometry

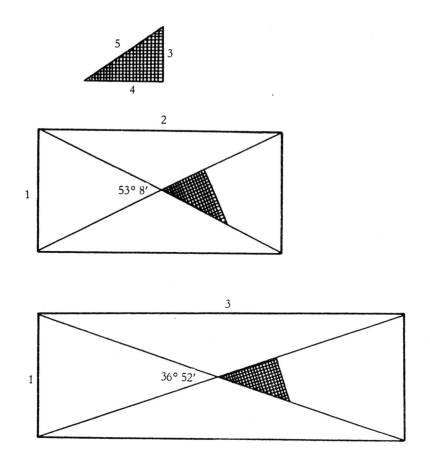

23. The medieval Mason's square, a 3, 4, 5 triangle. With this square, the double square may be laid out, using it as a 3:5 for the angle of the diagonals; and the triple square layout using the 4 and 5 sides of the square.

the patron of Amalfi is St Andrew. His reputed relics still reside there today, and his silver effigy holds a fish - the emblem of the vesica.

Although the peaceful traders of Amalfi imported the pointed arch, the other masonic secrets of Islam were not to be gained under the aegis of trade. On 27 November 1095 Pope Urban II appealed to Christendom to liberate the holy places of Palestine from the yoke of the Mohammedans and restore them to Christianity. Thousands of pious men, priests, monks, mercenaries, regular soldiers and opportunists rallied to the Pontiff's call. The First Crusade was startlingly successful. Nicaea was captured in 1097; the next year Antioch fell, and on 15 July 1099 the holy city of Jerusalem surrendered to the armies of Christendom after a mere six weeks' siege.

With this unprecedented success achieved, the 'Franks', as the Western Christians were known, proceeded to consolidate their conquests. As in England thirty years before, the conquered country was made secure for the new masters by the reinforcement of old castles and the construction of new ones at strategic points throughout the land. Naturally enough, the masons employed to build these castles used slave labour which doubtless included a proportion of Arab masons, for their designs incorporate several features which were hitherto unknown to European artificers.

The resilience and enthusiasm of the masons of that period are shown by the astonishing rapidity with which the new ideas swept Europe. The complex structure of the ribbed stone vault, known only in Persia and Armenia before the year 1100, was erected in the distant Durham Cathedral by 1104. In Wales, Neath Abbey was built by one of King Henry I's masons, Lalys, a Saracen prisoner-of-war. His techniques, learnt in the Middle East from a separate tradition, were no doubt transmitted to the English and Welsh masons who worked with him on the project.

Another important element in the new synthesis was the rediscovery of the works of the ancient Greek geometer Euclid. His work had been lost to Europe with the fall of the Roman Empire, and had survived only in Arabic translations. In about 1120, the English scholar Adelard of Bath made a translation of Euclid's *Elements* from Arabic into Latin, which made it accessible for the first time to European geometers and masons. The mode of transmission of this seminal work to England is not known, but the Knights Templar, who were the repository of much traditional arcane lore, may have obtained it from a conquered source. The Liverpool geometrician, Edward W. Cox wrote in 1890:

> During the period of the Crusades, many of the rules and mysteries that were known in Classic ages seem to have been re-organized. The influence of the occupation of Syria upon European architecture is most marked and wonderful. Not only were enormous numbers of churches, castles and other buildings erected in Palestine by the invaders with the help of skilled Syrian workmen, but the Templars and other military and religious orders, who founded establishments in Europe, brought with them this eastern knowledge.

Through the twelfth century and into the thirteenth century the early Gothic forms were developed and refined. Islamic methods were studied and incorporated into a new form-language which went hand-in-hand with an explosion of mystic symbolism. The great cathedrals of this era, like those at Chartres and Paris, appeared in a new complete form in a remarkably short time. Their construction, expedited with a literally religious fervour, still remains an astonishing feat of organization.

A separate but parallel tradition of church architecture was continuing at that time. Although they form a continuous if fragmented theme throughout the sacred architecture of the Christian world, round churches occupy a special and somewhat heretical place in the scheme of sacred geometry. The round edifice held a special place in Christian iconography for it was the form chosen for the Holy Sepulchre which marked at once the site of the tomb of Christ and the centre of the world. As the circular form of such buildings

The Comacines and Medieval Sacred Geometry

24. The round church at Little Maplestead, Essex, one of the four survivors intact in Britain.

represented the microcosmic reproduction of the world, so the round churches elsewhere represented local microcosms occupying the local geomantic omphalos.

Round churches originally were derived from earlier Pagan temples of the same form. The Roman round temples at Tivoli and Spalato, which have survived into modern times, are typical of the shrines which inspired the Christian sacred geometers. The former temple is based upon the Greek pattern, with external columnation, but the temple at Spalato, which was part of the palace complex of the staunch Pagan emperor Diocletian, had internal columns. This temple, planned on the octagon like many later Templar churches, formed the prototype for such early Christian shrines as San Vitale at Ravenna, which in turn was influential on both the original Holy Sepulchre in Jerusalem and Charlemagne's chapel.

Like the Pagan temples, the round churches were microcosms of the world. In the late Middle Ages, they became the prerogative of an enigmatic and heretical sect, the Knights Templar. This body was formed in 1118 in Jerusalem with the ostensible function of providing protection for pilgrims visiting the shrines of Christendom in the recently- conquered Holy Land. Their power rapidly grew, and before long the order became fabulously wealthy and was able to erect chapels and churches all over Christendom. The round form of church became especially connected with the order, and in the centre of the rotundae of their churches stood not an altar but a perfect cube of hewn stone which was one of the mysteries of Templarism.

The order was suppressed in 1314, and many of the highest ranking officials were sentenced to foul deaths by the church authorities. Their vast wealth found its way into the coffers of the monarchs of the country in which the order had functioned. But before the suppression, the fortune of the

Templars had enabled large numbers of round churches to be erected. John Stow, in *The Survey of London*, 1598, wrote; 'Many noble men in all parts of Christendom became brethren of this order, and built themselves temples in every city or great town in England, but this at London was their chief house, which they built after the form of the temple near to the sepulchre of Our Lord at Jerusalem; they also had other, temples in Cambridge, Bristow, Canterbury, Dover, Warwick.

There are now only six surviving round churches in the British Isles, two of which are now only fragmentary. The other four were extensively reconstructed during the last century. The churches at London, Northampton and Cambridge were built on the octagonal principle. That at Little Maplestead in Essex (which belonged to the Knights Hospitaller, sister organization of the Templars) was built on the hexagonal principle. On the Continent, the famous chapel at Drüggelte in Westphalia was made according to a twelve-sided plan, and the round church at Nijmegen in the Netherlands incorporated an eight- and sixteenfold structure. This church had a central octagon from which a sixteen-fold aisle was constructed by simple geometry.

At Altenfurt near Nürnberg in Germany was a church which represented the simplest form of round ecclesiastical architecture. This consisted of a round nave with a simple apse opposite the entrance. In the Orkneys, too, at Orphir, existed an almost identical round church known as the Girth House. It was largely demolished in the seventeenth century to provide materials for a new Presbyterian chapel nearby. It now exists as a fragment with only the apse still intact. However, its name gives us a clue to its microcosmic function. In Old Scottish, the word Girth or Gyrth had the meaning 'sanctuary' or 'asylum'. Girth, too was used to describe a circle of stones surrounding an ancient place of judgement. This infers that the round Orphir church may have replaced a stone circle formerly occupying its site. The word Girth is also cognate with garth and yarth, meaning earth, an overt description of the microcosm.

Round churches are in a separate tradition from the mainstream of ecclesiastical sacred geometry, having antecedents in Roman rather than Romanesque schemata. They were somehow special, reserved for important omphalos sites and not to be placed willy-nilly across the countryside. With the suppression of the Templars, the round form of church was effectively terminated until the Renaissance rediscovered the form directly from antique Pagan sources. Then it was soon to be again suppressed as its Pagan origin was soon recognized by the Church authorities.

Even as late as 1861, the round form was still considered Pagan. The Reverend J.L. Petit wrote in that year:

> Almost every continental specimen [of round church] is considered by the inhabitants of the place to have been a heathen temple; and, though in each particular instance it might seem needless to refute the supposition, yet the universality of the tradition might render it worth the notice of the antiquary. And if it is necessary to look for the derivation of so simple a form, there is no doubt that, like the rectangular form, it can be traced to the days of Paganism.

But why was the round form of church considered unchristian by the Church hierarchy? The round form, unlike other patterns such as the Latin Cross, did not represent the body of a man or the body of God. On the contrary, it represented the world, domain of earthly, and in Christian terms, satanic forces, the Devil in medieval times being personified as Rex Mundi, king of the world. In Templar usage, this worldliness was emphasized by the cube which stood at the very centre of the rotunda. The cube within the circle represented the earth within the heavens, the fusion of powers considered heretical by the medieval Christians, hence the persecution of the alchemists, magi and heretics who openly attempted such a fusion. With this open symbolism, it was not difficult to prove the accusations of heresy of which the unfortunate Templars stood accused. Overt Islamic principles, derived from the mystical wing of Mohammedanism, the Sufis, only served to further damn the sect.

However, Islamic knowhow was another matter. A second period of Islamic influence which was ultimately to sweep away the 'pure' Gothic of Chartres came about through a strange set of circumstances. During the thirteenth century the Mongol hordes expanded from their base in Central Asia and became a serious threat to the Middle East and Europe. After the first phase of expansion, the Mongol Empire was consolidated with its western outpost in Persia under the rule of a Viceroy who went by the title of Ilkhan. Having ceased to be a threat to Christendom, the Mongols were soon seen as allies against the Turks. Various Christian kings sent emissaries to successive Ilkhans in order to cultivate the alliance. Of especial note was the Ilkhan Arghun (1284-91) who had relations with several Christian states. He even sent an ambassador to London in 1289. In exchange, King Edward I of England sent a mission under Sir Geoffrey Langley to Persia. Langley had crusaded with the king in the early 1270s, and travelled to Persia by way of Contantinople and Trebizond in 1292. Such embassies were a channel for the transmission of new knowledge. Asian architects had blended their techniques with the Persian Islamic tradition and in turn their new style was transformed by European masons and geometers.

One building of the Ilkhan period which had a noticeable effect in Europe was the famed mausoleum of the Ilkhan Uljaitu at Sultaneih. At the beginning of this century, the German scholar Ernst Diez made an exhaustive study of this memorial. The whole structure is determined by two interpenetrating squares forming an octagon. From this basal octagon, the elevation containing both triangles and squares is derived. The height of the building, as measured by M. Dieulafoy in the 1880s, is 51 metres, and the internal diameter s exactly half this figure. A system of ratios, derived geometrically, was the basic origin of such harmonies. Whereas the mean diameter of the pillars had served the ancient Greeks as moduli, the Persian architects brought the dimensions of the arches or domes into determinate relationships with the other parts of the building. In Uljaitu's mausoleum, the basic point of departure was the dimension of the inner diameter of the burial chamber.

From this dimension the architect constructed an octagon for the ground plan. For the elevation, a double square was raised. Within the upper square, an equilateral triangle defined the dome and the drum upon which it was raised above the cubic basal portion. The side-chambers and galleries were determined geometrically by equilateral triangles whose positions were fixed by oblique squares and diagonals. The architecture of the mausoleum represented a constructional departure which in turn influenced the octagon at Ely Cathedral in the far-off fenlands of East Anglia. Mausolea with the roof as rafters of the dome had not appeared before in Persia, though they had been constructed in old Delhi. The same systems of geometry which the European masons utilized in their great buildings were used to glorify a quite different religious system. The oriental origin of such geometry, however, did not deter Christian architects in their task. Like progressive technologists, they welcomed the new ideas from the infidels and incorporated them in the latest works in hand. Transcendent principles were adopted with alacrity by pragmatic men whose grasp of symbolism had equipped them to deal with the untried and unexpected.

Accumulated knowledge from Persia and other Middle

Eastern countries was soon joined by information from further afield. In 1293, Christian missionaries from Italy reached China, and in 1295 Marco Polo returned to Venice from Peking. With such unprecedented interchange, new sacred geometries were inevitable. One well-documented example of oriental influence is in the Great Hall of the Plazza della Regione at Padua. This was designed by an Austin friar named Frate Giovanni in about 1306. Giovanni had travelled widely in Europe and Asia and had brought back plans and drawings of the buildings he had seen. At Padua, he reproduced a vast timber roof which he had seen in India, 240 by 84 feet.

Other oriental influences can be demonstrated by the simultaneous appearance of exotic themes in widely-separated places. The ogee arch, in which the arcs forming the arch are turned outwards and continued as an architectural feature above the door or window, appeared simultaneously without antecedent in both Venice and England. Details of the door at St Mary Redcliffe in Bristol and also the cathedral in that city and Berkeley Castle also show unmistakable oriental influence, which may be compared with the earlier work of Lalys at Neath.

The visits of such recorders of local architectural detail as Simon Simeon and Hugh the Illuminator to the Holy Land in 1323 served to reinforce the interest in monastic circles in oriental design. The 'Perpendicular' style in England which arose towards the end of the fourteenth century was foreshadowed by the elongated hexagons in Egyptian Muslim buildings of the thirteenth century. Vertical elements which cut through the curve of an arch, an important feature in the design of King's College Chapel in Cambridge (begun 1446) were already in existence in the Mausoleum of Mustapha Pasha in Cairo, built between 1269 and 1273. The masons of Europe, steeped in geometrical knowledge, readily assimilated the techniques of the symbolic architecture of Islam,

Sacred Geometry

enhancing it and bringing it through to a new era.

9. Masonic Symbolism and Documentary Evidence

Geometric lines speak the language of belief, strong, passionate, enduring belief. In them the eternal laws of proportion and symmetry reign supreme. The cycle of what is divinely generated is reproduced in the numerical language of choir, transept, nave, aisle, doorway, window, column, arcade, gable and tower. Every feature has its unit of measure, its mystic symbolism.

Hermon Gaylord Wood, *Ideal Metrology*

Medieval cathedrals are the finest flower of the art of sacred geometry which have risen in Europe. Physical manifestations of the summa theologiae, the microcosmic embodiment of the created universe, cathedrals in their perfect completed form, united in their position, orientation, geometry, proportion and symbolism, attempt to create the Great Work - the unification of man with God. Many cathedrals, such as Canterbury, Gloucester and Chartres, have been shown to have been built on the site of ancient megalithic circles, incorporating in their designs the positioning and geometry of the circles. Geomantically sited so that they might employ to the best the telluric energies of the earth and the astro-physical influences of the heavens, the stone circles overthrown by zealous Christian saints were amalgamated into the very fabric of the churches which succeeded them.

Sacred Geometry

Louis Charpentier made the suggestion that the ancient stones of megalithic structures in addition to absorbing cosmic and telluric influences acted as instruments of vibration. These stone instruments, he claimed, could accumulate and amplify the vibrations of the telluric waves, acting rather like a resonant drum. These energies, taken over by the Christians, still required a resonator, and this was provided by the stone walls and vaulting of the cathedral.

If the geometry of stone circles and dolmens was dependent upon the wavelength of telluric energies, then the geometry, reproduced in a vast stone building, would act as a channel for the resonating energies trapped therein. The legends which surround the fixation of earth energies on the omphalos, and which are embodied in world-wide tales of dragon-slayers, reinforce this contention. In dragon-slaying myths, the solar hero transfixes the dragon with his sword or spear. In so doing, he anchors the Earth's wandering telluric energies at one site so that they can be contained and channelled for the use of the priesthood. In later times, the solar hero became identified with the Christian saints George and Michael.

Another indication of this phenomenon is the universal acceptance of canonical measure. In most cultures, the fundamental units of measure are held not to have earthly origins but to have been handed down from the Gods. The recipient of these sacred measures was a man or demi-god, often the legendary founder of the nation. These measures were then jealously guarded against profanation and alteration, and employed largely in the construction of sacred architecture. Thus we see the proportions naturally generated by geometry from the starting measure. If the cathedral were designed to act as a channel and resonator, no better dimensions could be chosen than ones based upon a natural harmonic system laid out in measures related directly to a telluric wavelength. The wavelength of local telluric energies, once determined by occult methods, could be enshrined in unchangeable sacred measures and would form a natural basis for the construction of instruments to manipulate those energies.

Charpentier believed that the Benedictines stepped up the terrestrial forces by means of physical sound - Gregorian music - whose action enhanced the building's geometrical harmony to produce higher states of consciousness. The Benedictines were indeed one order which utilized ancient knowledge. The German researcher Kurt Gerlach found that the Benedictine monasteries in Bohemia (Czech Republic) had been arranged in precise geometrical relationships with one another. These monasteries were placed on lines at specific multiples and submultiples of the ancient measure known as the Raste, forty-four kilometres.

Thus the various characteristics of the Gothic cathedral were harmonized to create a whole which linked man the microcosm with the universe at large. The multiple functions expected of Gothic cathedrals meant that they could not merely be expressions of simple geometric harmony like Saint Chapelle in Paris or King's College Chapel in Cambridge. They needed various divisions and subdivisions in order to fulfil the functions of meeting- place, parish church, chantry, confessional and the seat of the local Bishop. In addition to these exoteric uses, the cathedral had to embody the doctrines of the faith and express the energies and geometries inherent in the site. Thus the geometries of Gothic cathedrals embody many complex structures which may be interpreted on a number of levels. The fundamental geometry of the ground plan is always generated directly from the orientated axial line. The date and position of the foundation is 'locked in, the geometry to the apparent solar position on the patronal day. Thus, on each successive patronal day, the sun would shine directly along the axis of the cathedral. Professor Lyle Borst made the discovery that several cathedrals have an east end geometry derived from stone circles. The orientations of these megalithic sites upon various solar and lunar phenomena are well known, having been researched by scholars such as Sir Norman Lockyer and Professor Alex Thom. The geometry of cathedrals, in overlaying that of the multiple orientations of the stone circles, must also preserve orientations other than the simple axial one of the patron's day. It may also mean that the patron may have been determined from the major orientation of the pre-existent stone circle.

At Angkor Wat in Cambodia, the layout of the vast temple complex was recently found to be designed in such a way t at twenty-two separate alignments of solar and lunar positions were incorporated. By watching the phenomena from certain well defined points, the astronomer-priest was able to check the calendar by direct observation. The construction of British cathedrals on top of megalithic observatories may have reproduced in a similar way the astronomical information in their geometry. Rose Heaword has shown that the Chapel of St Cross at Winchester has a sunrise alignment visible from a certain point through a window. This sunrise is on Holy Cross Day, 14 September, and is not the axial orientation of the chapel. Studies now underway may demonstrate more of these multiple alignments and their relationship to sacred geometry.

In the period in which the Gothic cathedrals were erected, there were two masonic systems of geometry in common use. The older was known as ad quadra turn and was based upon the square and its geometric derivatives. The younger, and in some respects more dynamic system, was based upon the equilateral triangle and was known as *ad triangulum.*

Ad quadratum was formed directly from the square and its derived figure, the octagram. The initial square, orientated in the manner approved by the geomancers and masons in charge of orientation, was overlain by a second square of the same size. This, at an angle of 45 degrees to the first square, formed the octagram, an eight-pointed polygram. In masonic tradition, this figure was invented by a master of Strasbourg, Albertus Argentinus. In later German masonic writings, this figure is called acht-ort or acht-uhr, eight hours or eight places. This name alludes to the ancient Pagan eightfold division of the compass, day and year which was echoed in the building as a microcosm of the world. From this initial octagram, the whole geometry of the church could be developed in one of two ways.

The first way, the true *acht-uhr*, developed a series of octagrams within and without, drawn directly from the first figure. Such systems may be seen at the cathedrals of Ely (see Figure 27), Verdun, Bamberg and many other basically Romanesque churches. However, by the time of the later Gothic churches, the system ad quadratum had become refined into a more complex form based upon the double rather than the single square. This form, it will be remembered, was favoured since Egyptian antiquity as a fitting shape for a holy enclosure.

The second and later derivation of *ad quadratum* produced the elegantly-proportioned geometrical complex known as the dodecaid, a twelve-pointed irregular polygram which lent itself admirably to church planning. Like the simple acht-uhr of the earlier *ad quadratum*, the basic figure was an octagram. However, the first square, from which the octagram was derived was itself extended to make a double square, and from this second square, another octagram was constructed. This made a figure of two contiguous squares with overlapping squares at 45^0 to the double square. Upon this interlaced octagram was superimposed a larger square which cut the inner intersections of the two octagrams. This produced a figure with intersecting in-built geometrical ratios.

The dodecaid is rich in Christian symbolism. The three overlapping squares have in their centre a small square common to all three. The central square is larger than the others, symbolizing the Father of the Christian Trinity, with the small square at the middle symbolic of the essential unity of the triune godhead. The frame of the double square which pervades the trinity, embodies the four elements and the four directions, symbolizing the material world interpenetrated and sustained by the godhead. The whole is a synopsis of the numbers three and four, the mystic seven.

In the actual fabric of the church, the four corners of the double square mark the four foundations of the church, the cornerstones upon which the material fabric is founded. The easternmost of the three 45^0 represents Christ. Its centre is the focus upon which the altar is founded, where, each day, through the celebration of the Mass, Christians believe, Christ is present in the form of the host and wine. The central and larger square, to the west, represents the father. It is based upon the central *omphalos*, the point at the crossing over which the main tower and spire would stand. This very centre, the overlapping point of the three squares representing the fusion of the trinity, often marked a powerful geomantic centre. This is discernible by dowsers in the form of a powerful blind spring with its associated spirals. Such a geomantic omphalos exists at Salisbury Cathedral, which has the tallest spire in England and marks a spot on a ley line from Stonehenge to Frankenbury. Further west of the central cross is the square which represents the Holy Ghost. Here, traditionally, stood the font, the place where the Holy Ghost entered the neophyte at his or her baptism.

The essence of sacred geometry is simple. All parts of the sacred ensemble from the apparatus and vestments of the clergy to the form of the whole sacred enclosure are determined directly from one fundamental geometrical figure. All dimensions and positions arc ideally related directly to this system and in so being are integrated with the whole of creation. The elevations of medieval churches were determined directly from the geometry of the ground plans.

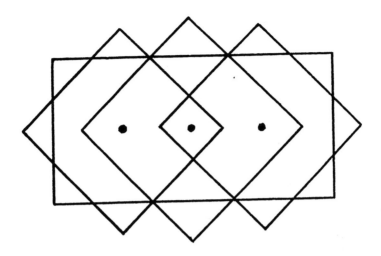

25. The Dodecaid, based on the double square.

Sainte Chapelle, the chapel of the French kings, admirably demonstrates this geometrical necessity. Its ground plan is produced by the dodecaid, with a small side-chapel from a smaller version of ad quadratum, and its internal elevational geometry directly from this. Later buildings, like King's College Chapel, were planned by the same methods, but dimensions instead of direct geometry were given in the authorizations of their plans. Thus the height of the vaulting at King's College was maintained in the finished chapel even though a different method of vaulting from that originally intended was installed.

Medieval churches were not designed merely as sheds to accommodate a certain number of worshippers; neither, as is often inferred, were they built 'as they went along'. Just as in modern architectural practice, everything was worked out in advance to the last detail, each and every feature of the building was determined exactly according to sacred geometry.

Sacred Geometry

Surviving records show concern in the minds of the designers with precise dimensions and proportions.

The ground plan of Ely Cathedral in Cambridgeshire will serve to illustrate the practical workings of medieval sacred geometry. Like many such buildings, the present cathedral is the result of many centuries of accretions. The original Norman cathedral was laid out in 1082 and completed about a century later. In the thirteenth century, a galilee porch was added. This was at the west end, the same position as those at Glastonbury and Durham. At the same time, an eastward extension of the chancel was made, its dimensions defined according to the principles of ad quadra turn. The extension was defined by one oblique square of nave width plus a 450 triangle of vault width. This oblique square was later used to determine the width of the new Lady Chapel, which was begun in 1321.

The dimensions of the Lady Chapel were not defined by *ad quadratum* turn, but by the newer masonic ad triangulum. Its dimensions were produced by the geometry of a circle whose radius is a little less than 105 statute feet (96 Saxon feet). This is the radius which defined the basic octagram from which the cathedral's ground plan is laid out. The internal corner of the north-east of the Lady Chapel is produced by intersecting radii of the same length, as is the north-west corner, which is also marked by the oblique square. The diagonal line which defines the eastern extent of the cathedral meets the north-west corner of the Lady Chapel after passing through the door into the chapel. A radius from the centre of the crossing which touches the end buttresses of the chancel's east end also touches the end buttresses of the Lady Chapel. Its radius is 192 Saxon feet - double the basic radius of the octagram, generated by ad quadratum geometry.

In the year after the commencement of the Lady Chapel, disaster struck. The central tower over the crossing collapsed towards the east, perhaps weakened by the building operations. Reconstruction commenced, and the original sacred geometry of *ad quadratum* was followed. The old tower was not copied, but a new octagon, a Gothic dome unprecedented in Western architecture, was erected in its stead. The technical method of construction was an almost exact copy of that used in the Persian mausoleum of the Uljaitu Chodabendeh at Sultaneib. Above this unprecedented stone octagon was constructed an incomparable wooden 'lantern', designed and executed by the Royal Carpenter, William Hurley. At its very centre is a magnificent carving of Christ in Majesty executed by John Burwell. Directly above the crossing, it represents the celestial counterpart of the earthly *omphalos* below it.

Although there is little surviving documentation on late Romanesque or early Gothic constructions, documentary details of two outstanding late medieval collegiate churches are still extant. Both the church of Fotheringhay in Northamptonshire and King's College Chapel in Cambridge were built according to precise instructions which still survive.

Both buildings were designed in the fifteenth century. Fotheringhay is the earlier of the two. The village of Fotheringhay is now remarkable only for its picturesque setting amidst the water meadows of the River Nene and the striking octagonal tower of a church whose outstanding design shows its former eminence. The isolated form of the church forlornly reminds us that it is now a mere fragment of a Royal college, now reduced to parish status. The college was founded by Edward Plantagenet, surnamed Langley, the fifth son of the occult-minded King Edward III. Edmund, Duke of York, was destined to be the founder of the House of York. He initiated the construction of the college and rebuilt the existing parish church, which was connected to it by a cloister of 88 windows of coloured glass. Edmund's son, Edward, Duke of York, wished to continue the project after his father's death

Sacred Geometry

26. The octagon of Ely Cathedral - the *omphalos* marker showing Christ in majesty.

by reconstructing the nave of the old church in the same style as the new choir, but he was slain in the Battle of Agincourt before building could commence. However, the project was not abandoned, and it is from an agreement signed on 24 September, 1434 that we draw evidence of the design practices of the English freemasons of that time.

The contract was made between William Wolston, Squire, and Thomas Pecham, clerk, commissioners for 'The high and mighty prince, my right dread Lord, the Duke of York', and William Horwood, Freemason of Fotheringhay. The contract detailed with precise measurements the specification for a church whose exquisite proportions still delight the eye today. The contract stipulated the making of 'a new nave of a church joining to the choir, of the College of Fotheringhay, of the same height and breadth that the said choir is; and in length eighty feet from the said choir downward, within walls a meter-yard [in thickness], a meter-yard of England, counted always as three feet ... And in the north side of the church the said William Horwood shall make a porch; the outer side of clean ashlar, the inner side of rough stone, containing in length twelve feet, and in breadth as the buttress of the said nave will permit ... and to the west end of the said nave shall be a steeple standing [above] the church upon three strong and mighty arches vaulted with stone. The said steeple shall have in length eighty feet after the meter- yard of three feet to the yard, above the ground from the table- stones and twenty feet square within the walls

Every detail of the proposed building was put down in the contract, with dimensions where relevant. Whether Horwood himself devised the dimensions and drew a diagram from which the contractual dimensions were taken is not known. Evidence from a mere twelve years later relating to another Royal collegiate foundation points to the design being laid down by the founder or his close aides in the geomantic field. Whatever the truth may be, the tone of the contract throughout is couched as instructions to Horwood, the functionary freemason who was merely carrying out orders from a higher authority, not details arbitrarily worked out by him.

Although Fotheringhay church was probably completed by 1460, the date of Richard Duke of York's death, the vaulting beneath the tower bears the stamp of the great master John Wastell, whose identical vaulting survives today at Peterborough Cathedral, the gateway of St John's College in Cambridge, and, above all, the masterly ceiling of the Chapel of King's College in the same city.

Sacred Geometry

27. Fotheringhay church tower.

The Comacines and Medieval Sacred Geometry

28. The roof of King's College Chapel, Cambridge.

This chapel was designed by King Henry VI, the founder. In his will of intent, dated 1448, he furnished all the dimensions necessary for his master mason, Reginald Ely, to prepare full plans for the chapel and indeed the whole college. Analysis of his plans show that they were based upon ad triangulum. Each part of the chapel is related to the overall geometry, even the small side chantries. Although sixty-nine years elapsed before the chapel was completed, the master mason John Wastell, who was not even born when the chapel was started, adhered to the letter of Henry's will in finishing it exactly to the dimensions stipulated. The geometrical system, despite alterations in dynastic and stylistic characteristics, was maintained as a sacred duty.

10. Problems, Conflicts and Divulgence of the Mysteries

Ancient history is like a night-landscape, over which we grope, vaguely discerning a few outlines in the general gloom, and happy if here or there the works of a particular author or a ruin or work of art momentarily illumine, like a lightning flash in the dark, the particular field which we are exploring.

Philo, *On The Contemplative Life*

The case of the construction of Milan Cathedral is of extreme importance in the study of sacred geometry. This is of interest on two counts, documentary and symbolic. Milan Cathedral was founded as late as 1386, and because of this was at the centre of a bitter controversy concerning which form of sacred geometry was to be used: ad quadratum or ad triangulum. A large number of experts was gathered together at the beginning in order to determine what should be done in the construction of this potential masterpiece. Perhaps because of this plethora of experts, a bitter argument developed between the protagonists of one system and the other.

As early as 1321 it is recorded that during the erection of the dome of the cathedral at Siena, the five inspectors appointed to examine the bullding objected to the continuance of the

Problems, Conflicts and Divulgence of the Mysteries

work 'because if complete as it had been begun it would not have that measure in length, breadth and height, which the rules of a church require.' A similar dispute arose with the construction of Milan Cathedral.

Today, Milan Cathedral stands as a masterpiece of late Gothic architecture. Recently, its fabric has been somewhat shaken by the vibrations of passing cars, trams and underground trains, but its early gestation was so fraught with recriminations that it seemed it might never have been completed. The cathedral was founded in 1386 on the orders of Gian Galeazzo Visconti, who had just achieved ascendancy in the city of Milan by the expediency of murdering his uncle. However, no such great building had been constructed in Lombardy for centuries, and soon the inexperienced masons in charge of the project ran into serious trouble. The theoretical side of the sacred geometry to which the building ought to be constructed became bogged down in a seemingly insoluble argument.

Initially, the ground plan of the cathedral had been laid out according to *ad quadratum*, based on the square and the double square, with an accentuated central nave and aisles of equal height. This, however, was soon given up and replaced by ad triangulum for the elevation, and this is where the problems started. The height of an equilateral triangle, the basis of ad triangulum, is incommensurable with its side. Put upon a ground plan of ad quadra turn, this would make nonsense of the commensurability of sacred geometry, and the whole proportions of the elevation would be totally wrong.

In order to get some semblance of logic back into the geometry, a mathematician, Gabriele Stornaloco from Piacenza was called in. He recommended the rounding-off of the incommensurable height of 83.138 to 84 braccia, which could then be conveniently divided into six units each of 14 braccia. Although acceptable in principle, Stornaloco's scheme was further modified, producing a further reduction in height and bringing the cathedral closer to Classical principles. The German master mason Heinrich Parler was infuriated by this compromise of true measure. His protests led to his dismissal from the post of consultant in 1392. In 1394, Ulrich von Ensingen came from Ulm as consultant, but stayed only six months before packing his bags. The Lombardic masons struggled on unassisted until 1399, when Jean Mignot was called in from France to oversee the works.

Mignot, however, did not last long either. His criticisms of local masonic principles were so vitriolic that a major meeting was called to discuss the points he raised. Such an ignorance of Gothic geometrical and mechanical principles was shown by the Lombardic masons that they attempted to argue that pointed arches exerted no thrust in justification for their aberrant geometry. Exasperated, Mignot spat 'Ars sine scientia nihil est' (Art without science is nothing). To this, he received the Lombardic retort 'Scientia sine arte nihil est' (Science without art is nothing).

Mignot returned to Paris in 1401, having made no progress with the intransigent Lombards. By pragmatic methods, the Italians soldiered on and finished the choir and transepts by about 1450. The whole cathedral was not finished, however, until the west front was finally completed at the orders of the Emperor Napoleon I in 1809. Milan's geometry was preserved in an edition of Vitruvius published in 1521. It shows the plan and elevation of the cathedral as an illustration of Vitruvian principles. This alone is evidence of the essential unity of the Classical and masonic systems of sacred geometry. The scheme shown in the engraving is based upon the rhombus or vesica. The triangular elevation of the cathedral's cross-section is shown superimposed upon concentric circles in which the square and hexagon are drawn, demonstrating the elevation's relationship with the ad quadratum of the basal plan.

This expose of the masonic sacred geometry of a cathedral is indicative of the changed attitude towards the ancient mysteries exhibited by writers of the Renaissance. It is directly in the tradition of Matthäus Röriczer, a mason who revealed his art by breaking his oath of sworn secrecy. Röriczer, who died in 1492, was of the third generation of a family which served as master masons at Regensburg Cathedral. Matthäus was the head of a lodge where all the building work was designed and executed, and as such was responsible for all mouldings and carvings, their layout and design. Although as a freemason he was bound by a horrendous oath never to divulge the masonic mysteries to the uninitiated, he made the unprecedented step of actually publishing details which formerly had been hidden in the private notebooks of operative masonic lodges.

Although Röriczer's only published work was a small pamphlet which gave the solution to a geometrical problem, it is of utmost importance because it is the only surviving key to masonic sacred geometry. The work, titled *On the Ordination of Pinnacles*, gave the solution to the problem of erecting a pinnacle of correct proportions from a given ground plan. As late as the end of the medieval period, masons were producing the masterworks of flamboyant and perpendicular Gothic by the simplest means. Working drawings (known in England as 'plats') were prepared by the master mason complete to the last detail. Such plats as the drawing for the west front of Strasbourg Cathedral, drawn by Michael Parler in 1385, and the spire of Ulm Cathedral by Mätthias Böblinger, are still in existence. Each part of the intricate design is related to its fellows through geometry. The operative mason, provided with such a diagram, could take one dimension as the starting-point, and from that by straightedge and compass geometry arrive at a full-size plan for the parts he was to make. From this full-size plan, drawn on a tracing floor' of plaster, wooden templates were made, according to which the final stones were cut and carved.

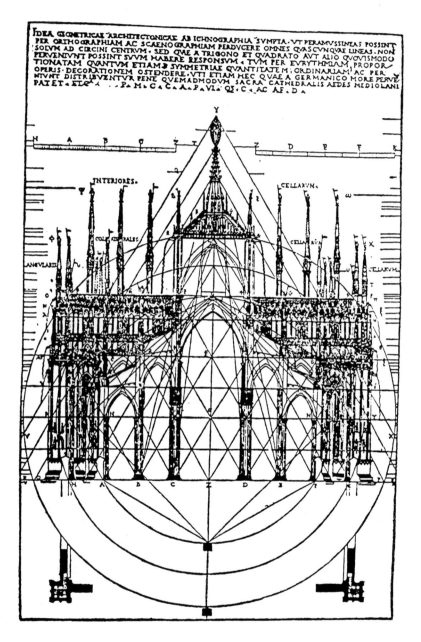

29. Caesariano's woodcut of the *ad triangulum* design of Milan Cathedral.

Röriczer's expose of the system admirably demonstrates the elegant simplicity of this canonical method. Instead of constant reference to measurements on a plan, as in modern engineering practice, the pinnacle (or mullion, door jamb, vault component etc.) was organically 'grown, as it were, from a square. Geometry, unlike measurement, is self-regulating and any mistakes are immediately apparent. Whatever the size of the initial square, all parts of the pinnacle are related to it in natural proportion. As the dimensions of the original square would have been derived as a function of the overall geometry of the church, the pinnacle's size was automatically related harmoniously to the whole.

Röriczer's booklet was dedicated to Prince Wilhelm, Bishop of Eichstadt (1464-96), who was described in the dedication as ... an amateur and patron of the free art of geometry'. Wilhelm was active in the building council of the churches at Regensburg, Ulm and Ingolstadt. From Röriczer's introduction, we find that Wilhelm was not merely an administrator, but was interested in knowing the exact methodology behind sacred geometry. Such men were the first of the 'speculative masons', wealthy patrons who genuinely wished to know the secrets of the functioning operative masons. In order to gain these secrets, the patrons were generally admitted to the brotherhood of the freemasons by way of the standard initiatory rites. As the activities of the masons waned with the rise of academically-trained architects, the number of speculative masons' increased.

Meanwhile, the operative lodges of freemasons closed down one by one. The last to go was the premier lodge of Europe - Strasbourg, which shut up shop in 1777. From then on, the arts and mysteries of freemasonry were carried on exclusively by 'speculative masons'.

The pinnacles described by Röriczer are constructed according to *ad quadratum*. Although *ad triangulum* was the late medieval German method of sacred geometry, it was not easily applicable to the finials and buttresses which are an integral part of Gothic construction. So *ad quadratum* was used in these essential parts of the fabric. The production of the plan of a pinnacle was as follows:

> Röriczer: 'Would you draw a plan for a pinnacle after the mason 5 art, by regular geometry? Then make a square as is here designated with the letters A:B:C:D: draw A to B and B to D and D to C and from C to A so it may be as in the given figure.
>
> Then you make another square. Divide A to B in two equal parts and place E; likewise divide BD and there make H; and from D to C and there make an F; similarly from C to A, and there make a G. After that draw a line from E to H and from H to F,F to G,G to E.
>
> After that you make like the one made above another square.
>
> After that you make the three squares equal to the size of ABC and IKLM and the square EHGF; these as in the given figure.'

These three squares bear a specific geometrical relationship to one another: the diagonal of the second square is equal to the side of the first square, and the diagonal of the third is equal to the side of the second. The next action in R5riczer's geometry involves the drawing in of the four corners; from this the radius IN is taken, and with a compass quadrants are drawn which produces the dimensions of the hollow moulding of the panel and the completed plan of the shaft. From this plan by a simple action of a ruler and compass the final ground plan of~a pinnacle was constructed.

Problems, Conflicts and Divulgence of the Mysteries

From this complex ground plan, the elevation was made by equally simple moves of compass and straightedge. The masons who carried out these works each possessed an individual mark which could be used to identify not only the work of the mason himself, but also the lodge from which he came. Masons' marks have existed in all countries in the Western architectural tradition from ancient Egypt onwards, and are characteristic sigils which usually have been derived geometrically.

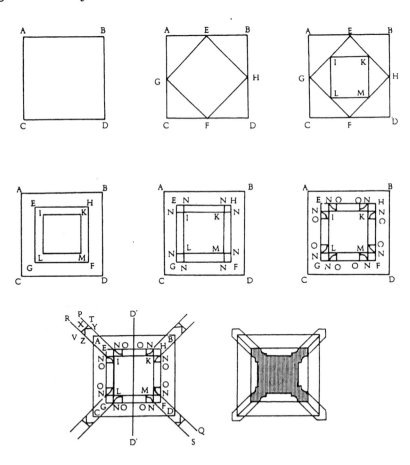

30. The pinnacle construction of Röriczer.

Sacred Geometry

Although a 'masonic secret', it has long been contended that each central lodge of operative masons each had its own 'mother diagram' from which were derived all the marks used by its members. Professor Homeyer, in Hof und Hausmarken, published in 1870, mentioned that in about the year 1820, a Dr Parthey had given him such a 'mother diagram' upon which were based all the marks of masons found in Strasbourg Cathedral. This diagram was said to have been discovered by a certain Arnold of Strasbourg, an architect.

In the year 1828 the mason Kirchner of Nürnberg is reported

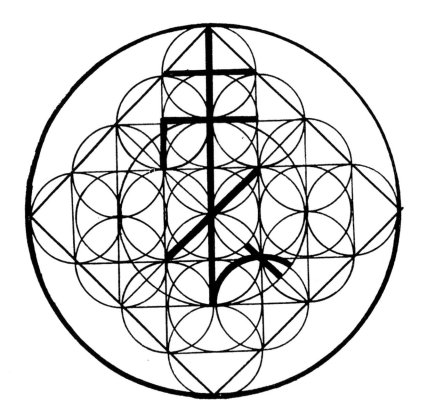

31. *Vierpasse*, 'mother diagram' of mason's marks, after Professor Rziha.

Problems, Conflicts and Divulgence of the Mysteries

MEDIEVAL SCOTTISH

SARACEN

EGYPTIAN

PERSIAN

MURISTANI

SYRIAN

JERUSALEM

MEDIEVAL ENGLAND

MEDIEVAL FRANCE

NINETEENTH CENTURY ENGLISH AND SCOTTISH

32. Selected mason's marks.

Sacred Geometry

as being in possession of a book which derived all the individual masons marks from a common source. Professor Franz Rziha in his work *Studien über Steinmetz-zeichen*, published in 1883 in Vienna, demonstrated that from certain fundamental geometrical diagrams may be derived a series of 'mother diagrams' or keys into which may be fitted all the masons' marks known. In the sixty-eight plates illustrating this work, Rziha fitted 1145 marks into their proper diagrams, demonstrating the universality of the system.

The knowledge of all levels of geometry was thus the prerogative of the freemason. From his knowledge of the marks' geometry, a mason could 'prove' his mark when required to do so, and could also judge the origin of any other mark he saw. Professor Rziha discovered four basic geometrical diagrams, upon which all masons marks were based. The first two diagrams were the standard *ad quadratum* and *ad triangulum* patterns. The other two were more complex, being dubbed by Rziha *vierpasse* and *dreipasse*. *Vierpasse* corresponded to the square geometry incorporating related vesicas, while *dreipasse* used a different combination of equilateral triangles and circles. Each of these diagrams is capable of any amount of extension, and a very elaborate series of geometrical figures thus forms the basis of masons marks.

Rziha found the 'mother diagrams' for a number of the major European centres of masonic knowledge, *inter alia* Nürnberg, Prague, Strasbourg, Vienna, Cologne and Dresden. The geometry of the macrocosm was reproduced to the smallest level within the European masonic tradition, and thus even the barely noticeable marks carved on individual stones were nevertheless emblematical of the transcendent structures of the universe.

11. Renaissance Sacred Geometry

God also created man after his own image: for as the world is the image of God, so man is the image of the world.

H. Cornelius Agrippa, *Occult Philosophy*

With the rediscovery of the old Classical Roman modes of architecture, the linear, overlapping geometry of the medieval period was rapidly superseded by a centralized polygonal geometry. In the fifteenth century in Italy a gradual transition can be seen in the plans of churches from the traditional Latin Cross to the centralized. This centralizing tendency, derived from antique pagan practice, has been seen by many historians as emblematical of a move away from the transcendent Christian beliefs of the Middle Ages towards a more humanist, anthropocentric ethos. This reductionist view that medieval Christian belief was swept away in an onslaught of ebullient atheist humanism ignores the underlying trends in the geometrical thought of the period.

Centralized churches posed the problem of the hierarchical separation of congregation and clergy, and, most fundamentally, the question of the site of the altar. The niceties of centralized geometry, however, were compelling. A key work in the understanding of this new geometry is the first architectural treatise of the Renaissance, *De re aedificatoria*, written between 1443 and 1452 by the architect Alberti. The Pagan origins of his ideas are shown most clearly in his designs for temples, as he calls churches. The circle, he asserts, is the primary form which above all others is favoured by nature, from the form of the world downwards. For temples, Alberti demonstrates the use of nine geometrical figures. He uses the circle, five regular polygons (the square, hexagon, octagon, decagon and dodecagon) and three rectangles (the square and a half, square and a third and double square).

From these basic ground plans, Alberti develops geometric appendages which serve as side-chapels. These are either rectangular or semicircular in form, and are related radially to the centre point. By the addition of simple geometrical figures to the basic polygon or circle, an almost infinite range of configurations may be produced.

Alberti was inspired by Vitruvian buildings of the Classical era, but, strangely, the central form which he favoured so much was uncommon in temples of that period. Only three round temples actually survived from Classical times, the celebrated Pantheon and two small peripteral temples at Tivoli and Rome. The vast majority of Classical temples were, of course, of rectangular plan. However, during the Renaissance, other polygonal buildings of antiquity, like the decagonal 'temple of Minerva Medica' in Rome, in reality the nymphaeum of the Orti Liciniani, and early Christian structures such as Sto. Stefano Rotondo and Sta. Constanza were looked upon as antique temples.

Vitruvius did not even include round buildings among the seven classes of temple enumerated in his Third Book, but instead mentioned them almost as an afterthought in Book Four along with the aberrant Tuscan form. However, Alberti's predilection for the polygonal form, influenced by the Platonic Solids, was justified on the pretext that it was a return to the liturgical simplicity of the Rome of Constantine. At that period, the Roman College of Architects was compelled to transfer its expertise from the design of temples for the Pagans to the creation of churches for the new official faith. The Constantinian period was especially potent for the Renaissance mind, as it was the unique meeting- point and fusion of fully-developed classical architecture with the pure faith of Imperial Christianity.

However, in Constantine's Rome, the normal form of churches was the basilica, a pattern derived from the Law Tribunals. Alberti does not approve this type of edifice, but mentions in passing that the early Christians used private Roman basilicas as places in which to celebrate their rites. The basilica, the seat of human justice, was related to religion in a symbolic manner: as justice was held to be the gift of God, the presence of God is forever within the sphere of juridical decisions, and hence the basilica is brought within the realms of worship.

The fundamentally human and functional plan of the basilica is held by Alberti to be too prosaic. It does not arouse a feeling of awe and piety in the beholder. It does not have the effect of purification which induces a state of primal innocence pleasing to God because it is not constructed according to sacred geometry. In Renaissance centralized churches, the geometrical form is explicit, unlike the arcane geometry underlying the basilica or Gothic church, a geometry only appreciable by the initiate. In a Renaissance plan, pure geometry is overwhelmingly dominant. Each part is related harmonically like the members of a body, making manifest the nature of divinity.

Like many of his contemporaries, Alberti wrote at length on the attributes of the ideal church. Like its related theme, the città ideale or ideal city, this church is an idealized expression of the cosmic absolute, designed as a visible manifestation of the divine harmony, in essence a Neoplatonic concept. Alberti's church was intended to stand on high ground, free on all sides in the centre of a fine piazza. It was to be based on a high plinth which served to shield it from the profanity of everyday life, and be surrounded by a colonnade in the manner of the ancient temples of Vesta.

Its explicit geometry was to be covered by a fine dome, which internally was to be panelled in coffers after the fashion of the Pantheon. The vault of the dome was also to bear a likeness of the sky, in the tradition of the universal cosmic interpretation of the temple. Thus, as in Eastern Orthodox architecture and Western Gothic, the whole round church was emblematical of the world - the created manifestation of the Word of God: a perfect vessel for humanity.

Like the round churches of the Templar period, such central churches were seen not only as microcosms of the world, but also as symbolic of the universality of God. Many centralized churches unconsciously revived the cosmic cube in the form of a central altar. The centre, the 'one and absolute', in Christian iconography is a reflection of Him who alone truly Is. Because his omnipresence was represented by the performance of the sacraments, the altar was at the centre, the *omphalos* upon which all the radii of the building were made to converge.

Many such centralized churches found their dedication in the Virgin Mary. This was not without symbolic reason. From the earliest period of the Christian religion, the cult of the mother of Christ saw her as queen of heaven and protector of the whole universe. These ideas arose out of the mythology associated with her burial, assumption and coronation, the circular crown of the heavenly queen echoing the age-old tradition of the circular heavens.

Circular churches were, however, to enjoy only a short-lived success. The greatest number were constructed in the period

1490-1560. Christianity was not going to give up its ancient traditions so easily. In the year 1483, an Italian artist, Domenico Neroni, his patron Ascanio de Vulterra and an unnamed priest were executed for sacrilege. Inspired with an overriding desire to know the Perfect Number and the proportions which guided the ancient sculptors in making effigies of the gods, they had conceived a scheme of evoking those gods. For performing acts of ritual magic, they were sentenced to death. The ancient proportions were so closely allied with Pagan religion, that it was only a matter of time before the Church rejected Alberti's 'temples' on the grounds of their Pagan origin. Such events as this case must have sown the seeds of doubt in the minds of the orthodox.

In 1554, Pietro Cataneo in his book I quattro libri ~di architettura reiterated the concept that the temple was symbolic of the body of God. He asserted that because of this, cathedrals ought to be dedicated to the crucified Christ and as such ought to follow the form of the Latin Cross. In 1572, Carlo Borromeo in *Instructionum Fabricae ecclesiasticae et Superlectilis ecclesiasticae* attacked the round form of churches as Pagan. Following the Council of Trent, he also recommended the use of the Latin Cross.

Although there was controversy and hints of heresy surrounding the use of round churches, the ancient proportional systems were considered admirable by the orthodox. A surviving document relating to S. Francesco della Vigna in Venice gives us an insight into the proportional system employed in the orthodox-shaped churches of the Renaissance. The Doge of Venice, Andrea Gritti, had laid the foundation-stone of the new church on 15 August 1534, and building had commenced to the designs of Jacopo Sansovino. But, as in the earlier troubles with Milan Cathedral, arguments had arisen over the proportional system to be employed. An expert on proportion, Francesco Giorgi, a Franciscan monk who in 1525 had published a treatise on the

Universal Harmony (*De Harmonia Mundi Totius*), was commissioned to write a commentary on Sansovino 5 plan. Giorgi's treatise had blended Neoplatonic and Christian theory which had the effect of reinforcing the already-existing belief in the efficacy of numerical ratio.

For this church, Giorgi suggested making the width of the nave nine paces, as it is the square of three. Three is the first real number in Pythagorean terms because it has a beginning, a middle and an end. The length of the nave was to be three times the width, the symbolic cube, 3 y 3 x 3, which, like the City of Revelation or the Jewish Holy of Holies contains the consonances of the Universe. The width to length ratio of 9:27 is also analyzable in musical terms, forming a diapason and diapente (an octave and a fifth). Giorgi thus suggested the progression of the male side of the Platonic triangle for the nave of the church.

At the eastern end of the church, the chapel was to be nine paces in width and six in length, representing the head of Vitruvian Man. In length, this chapel repeated the nave s width and in width it had the ratio 2:3, a diapente. The choir, too, repeated the eastern chapel's dimensions, making the whole church 5 x 9 = 45 paces in length, a disdiapason and diapente in musical terms. The chapels on either side of the nave were three paces wide, and the transept six paces. The ratio of the width of the chapels of the transept to that of the nave was 4:3, a diatessaron. The height of the ceiling was also to bear a relationship of 4:3 with the width of the nave.

This overall system, related to the ideal proportions of Vitruvian Man and to the cosmic harmonies of Plato and Pythagoras, was received with pleasure, and implemented, after being passed by the painter Titian, the architect Serlio and the Humanist philosopher Fortunio Spira. The church facade was completed by Palladio thirty years later, according to the same system of proportion and harmonic ratios.

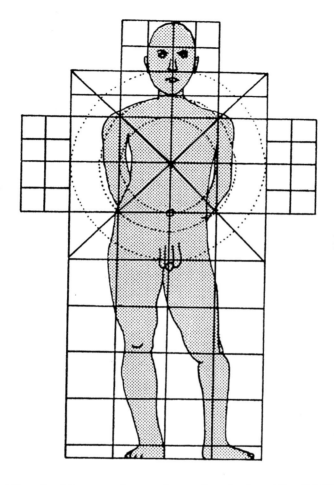

33. Vitruvian Man superimposed on a church plan. After Di Giorgio.

Palladio was one of the greatest exponents of Renaissance sacred geometry. In his influential book *Quattro libri dell'architettura*, Andrea Palladio attempted to produce a survey of the whole of architecture. He naturally stressed his debt to Vitruvius, and also to Alberti. However, it was to Vitruvius that Palladio owed his greatest inspiration. To him, Vitruvius held the key to the mysteries of ancient architecture, its systems of proportion and occult symbolism. But Palladio did not merely possess an academic knowledge of Classical architecture. He had travelled round Italy visiting the remains of these buildings and producing detailed measured drawings in order to verify Vitruvian statements.

Palladio wrote, 'Although variety and things new may please everyone, yet they ought not to be done contrary to the precepts of art, and contrary to that which reason dictates; whence one sees, that although the ancients did vary, yet they never departed from some universal and necessary rule of art.' With this axiom in mind, Palladio proceeded to reinterpret the ancient Classical sacred geometry in the design of his memorable buildings. Palladio's villas were designed with a rigid symmetry derived from a single geometrical formula. The rooms together with their porticos are based upon a rectangle divided by two longitudinal and four transverse lines. His rightfully most famous work is the Villa Rotondo, a masterly design which spawned many inferior imitations. In plan, the design is more fitting for a religious building, as it is of obvious cosmic origin. In essence, it is composed of the quartered square of earth supporting the circular dome of heaven. In all of Palladio's buildings, harmonic ratios are employed inside each room and in the relationship of each room to each other. The old sacred geometry of Pagan temples had been refined into a system for the palatial residences of the wealthy.

Palladio had a profound influence on Renaissance architecture, and later, in England, Inigo Jones popularized his style. In his Quattro Libri, Palladio alludes to a general system of proportion which he used in all his commissions. He details what he considers the most harmonious proportions for width-to-length ratiOs of rooms. Like Alberti's churches, Palladio's work recommends the mystic seven forms of rooms: circular, square, the diagonal of the square for the room's length ($\sqrt{2}$), a square and a third, a square and a half, a square and two thirds and the double square. The ratios recommended are thus: 1: 1:1; √2: 1; 3:4; 2:3; 3:5; and 1:2. The third is the only incommensurable in this progression, and is the only irrational number generally found in Renaissance sacred geometry. It appears in Vitruvius amidst a commensurable system, and as such probably represents the last vestige of the ancient Greek sacred geometry, surviving as a fragment into the Roman period.

Palladio states that there are three different groups of ratios which give good proportions for rooms, for each three he gives a mode of calculation for heights based both on a geometrical and arithmetical method. Suppose a room measures 6 x 12 feet (the double square), then its height must be 9 feet. If it is 4 X 9 feet, its height must be 6 feet. In the arithmetic method, the second term exceeds the first by the same amount as the third exceeds the second. In the geometric method, the first is to the second term as the second is to the third. Another, more complex example, is given: the harmonic method.

For a room 6 x 12, the height by the harmonic method will be 8 feet. This geometrical method was according to the idea of harmonics expounded in Plato's Timaeus, being 'the mean exceeding one extreme and being exceeded by the other by the same fraction of the extremes'. In the progression 6:8:12, the mean exceeds 8 by 6 by 1/3rd of 6, and is exceeded by 12 by 1/3 rd of 12.

Palladio probably took this idea directly from the works of Alberti, but it had also been treated by Giorgi in Harmonia Mundi and by Ficino in his commentary on the Timaeus. It is, of course, grounded directly in Classical musical theory, and as such comes directly from the Harmony of the Spheres, the mystic pulse of the Universe recognized by pagan and magician alike. This idea is common to the Renaissance and the medieval period, but it was during the later period that it was formalized in the commentary of Ficino and such works as De Musica by Boethius.

The use of musically-derived harmonies in architecture was held to be expressive of the Divine Harmony engendered at the act of creation by God, in modern terms, the 'echo' of the Big Bang which began the Universe. Through this expressiveness of the Divine Harmony, the dual symbols of the temple as the body of Man the Microcosm and the temple as the embodiment of the totality of creation were integrated. In De Sculptura, published in 1503, the author Pomponius Gauricus asks the question 'What geometrician, what musician must he have been who has formed man like that?' Gauricus, again, largely based his theories on Plato's *Timaeus*.

The explicit connection between visual and audible proportions in the Renaissance again brings up the possibility that it may have been derived initially from the need to construct temples as instruments which could channel telluric energies. In Pythagorean-Platonic thought, music itself was seen as an expression of the Universal Harmony, and it was an essential part of an architect's training. The great Renaissance architects from Brunelleschi onwards avidly studied the music of the ancients. Architectural aberrations were seen in terms of musical discord, and such alterations of the system of proportion would mean that the temple could no longer act as an instrument for the production of the Divine Harmony. For example, during the construction of the church of S. Francesco at Rimini, Alberti warned Matteo de Pasti that in altering the proportions of the pilasters 'all the musical relationships are destroyed'.

Writers like Lomazzo constantly refer to the human body in terms of musical harmony. For instance, the distance between the nose and the chin and that from the chin to the meeting of the collar bones is a diapason. Lomazzo, in his Idea del Tempio della Pittura, published in 1590, asserts that the masters like Leonardo, Michelangelo and Ferrari came to the use of harmonic proportion through the study of music. Lomazzo mentions how the architect Giacomo Soldati added to the three Greek and two Roman orders a sixth, which he called Harmonic. Soldati was an engineer who was mainly involved with the construction of hydraulic machines, and so was adept at handling the geometrical knowledge necessary to create a sixth order of architecture. Unfortunately, no drawings of this sixth order survive, neither are there any known buildings in the style. However, the sixth order was intended to encompass all the qualities inherent in the original five orders and express more forcefully the basic oneness and harmonious patterns of the Universe.

The sixth order was believed to be the recreation of the lost order of the Temple at Jerusalem, which was inspired directly by Jahweh when he ordered Solomon to build it according to preordained measures. The Pagan allegations of the orthodox were silenced. The total orthodoxy of the Temple of Solomon, directly ordained by God, was the precedent for the application of the harmonic ratios of sacred geometry in Christian edifices. The reconstruction of the much-destroyed Temple also became the aim of many architects in that period. Like Soldati, the Spanish jesuit Villalpanda was interested in the recovery of the sixth order. H is researches led to a new generation of design. Perhaps the most impressive and complex work occasioned by the theories concerning the Temple at Jerusalem was El Escorial, the stupendous palace-monastery erected on the orders of King Philip II of Spain. The foundation of the Monastery of San Lorenzo of El Escorial, to give it its full name, was conceived as an act of thanksgiving for the Spanish victory in the battle of San Quentin.

El Escorial was built as the direct result of a holy vow which Philip II made on the eve of the battle. Fought on St Lawrence 5 Day, 10 August 1557, the battle resulted in the defeat of the French by Philip's forces. In recognition of this momentous day, the axis of the church of the Escorial and hence the entire geometrical pattern of the monastery was oriented upon the point of sunset for 10 August. This is extremely unusual, as sunrise was and is almost universally acknowledged as the correct time of day for the determination of such alignments.

The general plan of the building, in gridiron form, is said to recall the appalling martyrdom of the patron saint, of whom the King was a devotee. Philip decided to build this massive monastic settlement for the Hieronymite Order, and planned it according to Biblical revelations. The work of construction commenced on 23 April 1563, and took twenty-one years to complete. The architect Juan Bautista de Toledo was commissioned to direct the work, but on his early death his assistant Juan de Herrera took over and accomplished a magnificent sacred edifice in a very personal style. Nevertheless, despite his personal stamp, the principles adhered strictly to the canonical. Both Philip II and Juan de Herrera were ardent followers of the Spanish mystic Ram6n Lull, whose mathematical expositions of the Universal Harmony had earned him the death penalty for anti-Islamic heresy during the Moorish occupation.

Herrera had previously applied musically-derived harmonies in his construction of the cathedral at Valladolid, and proceeded to do the same with the Escorial. Basically Vitruvian in design, the overriding geometry is the ad triangulum. The whole ground plan is analyzed as encompassing Vitruvian Man. In overall planning, the Escorial echoes the Camp of the Israelites, a theme taken up by Villalpanda in his learned treatise on Ezekiel. As the image of the macrocosom, the monastery was founded on a day astrologically and historically favourable, and was intended from the first to be the epitome of the arts and letters of the era.

Problems, Conflicts and Divulgence of the Mysteries

The milieu in Spanish mystical circles at the time of the Escorial's foundation produced a monumental work, *In Ezechielem Explanationes*. Although actually published after the completion of the monastery, it gives the key to the ideas inextricably involved in it. Two Jesuits Juan Bautista Villalpanda and Jeronimo Prado, carried out over an extended period a series of complex and painstaking researches into the structure and symbolism of the Temple of Solomon and its interpretation in the vision of Ezekiel. The reconstruction, and the reasoning behind it, occupies most of the second of three tomes commenting on the *Book of Ezekiel*. These were financed by Philip II, to whom the first volume is dedicated. The dedication says he 'resembled ... Solomon in greatness of soul and wisdom as in building the most magnificent and truly Royal works of St Lawrence of the Escorial.' This fancied resemblance to Solomon echoes the selfsame allusions applied to the Eastern Roman Emperor Justinian and the Holy Roman Emperor, Charlemagne. Codimus relates that Justinian, on seeing the great church of Santa Sophia in Constantinople exclaimed 'Solomon, I have surpassed you!' and Charlemagne, according to his biographer Notker the Stammerer, built his churches and palaces 'following the example of Solomon'. Furthermore, one of the titles carried by Philip II was King of Jerusalem, and the Escorial was modelled upon that very temple.

According to Villalpanda, the Platonic harmony used by Alberti, Palladio and Soldati, had been revealed to Solomon by God. The system utilizes the musical harmonies of diatessaron, diapason, diapente, diapason cum diapente and disdiapason, but rejects the Vitruvian sixth consonance of diapason cum diatessaron. By these means, the complex relationship of the elements of Classical architecture were related to the Will of God.

This vast mystical work was extremely widely read and very influential, in that it synthesized the eschatological mysteries of the Old Testament with the Platonic Graeco-Roman architectural theories of Vitruvius. Herrera, the architect so intimately connected with the execution of Philip II's wishes, is referred to by Villalpanda as his master. As a disciple of Herrera, Villalpanda was in a perfect position to expound the occult principles which underlie the Escorial and its predecessor, the Solomonic Temple. His reconstruction can be dated to 1580, sixteen years before publication, and Herrera, on seeing the drawings, is said to have commented that a building of such beauty could only have come from God.

Villalpanda and Prado were not the first commentators to attempt a perfect reconstruction of the Solomonic Temple. In fact, the first and perhaps most famed librarian of the Escorial, Benito Arias Montano, had published in 1572 his own interpretation of the Temple. This was in a totally Classical style with a four-staged tower in the Renaissance manner. Villalpanda dismissed this as fantasy because it 'did not follow the specification of Holy prophecy, not even in part'. Villalpanda, a vastly erudite Biblical scholar and Hebraist, believed that he had, through the spiritual exercises of his order, come to the true manifestation of the Temple. His mystical, indeed occult, roots were in the Hebrew Qabalah, the Pagan Canon of Vitruvius and the mathematical mysticism of the heretical Ramón Lull.

The Temple's precincts, often ignored by later reconstructors, especially those of the Protestant persuasion, were of utmost importance for Villalpanda. Enclosed in the general form of a square, the seven courts astrologically represented the seven planets, and other significant points the astrological houses and the tribes of Israel.

Not all mystical buildings of the period went back to Biblical sources for inspiration. A unique building in England which overtly displays both sacred geometry and occult mathematics is the famed Triangular Lodge at Rushton, Northamptonshire.

This devotional building was erected on the orders of Sir Thomas Tresham, a devotee of Roman Catholicism who wished to continue his private worship in a political climate hostile to that religion. The Triangular Lodge was his expression of his devotion to the Holy Trinity, and, being emblematical of the Trinity, is in the form of an equilateral triangle.

Each side of the lodge is 33 feet 4 inches in length. There are three floors; three windows in each storey on each of the three sides, each window being divided into three. There are three Latin inscriptions, each of which has thirty-three letters. One however is the ampersand which makes the round hundred notable in the total length of the sides. The roof is finished with three gables a side, and a three-sided finial surmounts the roof. Below the windows of the second storey on the entrance side are the date 1593 and the initials of the builder, T.T. Even the letter 'T' is symbolic of three.

The ornament, if it can be called that, is deeply occult in content. On one gable are the figures 3898 and beneath them the *Menorah*, the seven-branched candlestick of the Jews. On the next gable, there is the inscription *Respicite*, and a sundial. On the third gable is the number 3509 and the stone with seven eyes upon it. Each of the three sides thus represents one aspect of the Trinity. The lodge remains an oddity, though a triangular church emblematical of the Holy Trinity was erected in Bermondsey in London as late as 1962. Triangular buildings are notoriously impractical for either accommodation or worship, so very few have been countenanced. Sacred geometry allows for this, and enables the architect to incorporate the symbolism in an arcane manner. Tresham bypassed the traditional method and made a memorable 'folly' - but one which stands as witness to an extraordinary religious fervour.

Sacred Geometry

34. Renaissance magical sigil showing various levels of power.

At about the same period, magic, shorn of its heretical label and practised under the new order of Rosicrucianism, began to openly flourish in Protestant England, and polymaths like John Dee and Robert Fludd, whose researches ranged from mathematics to alchemy by way of astrology and occultism, created various systems of sacred geometry with which to encode their magical discoveries.

12. Baroque Geometry

The Baroque is applied nowadays to the architecture of the seventeenth and eighteenth centuries, having been originally a term of abuse derived from the Italian word *Baroco*. This word was used by the philosophers of the Middle Ages to describe any overcomplex idea or involuted concept. It was also applied to anything bizarre or misshapen, for example a pearl, and inferred the breaking of the canonical rules of proportion at the whim of the artist or architect. Thus, Baroque, like the later Art Nouveau movement, was seen by purists as degenerate for its departure from the more or less rigid canon of Classical architecture.

Baroque architecture may be seen as a continuation of the Classical revival of the Renaissance. Indeed, the earliest buildings in the Baroque style are directly in the tradition and may be distinguished only by detail differences in the handling of ornament. However, the Baroque proper represents a complete break with the ordered style of Roman architecture, and this is reflected in its underlying geometry.

It is often erroneously stated that in Classical sacred geometry the forms of buildings must be simply related to the major geometrical figures. In the Baroque we see the first departure from this concept, for, although the forms are related to the familiar geometrical figures, they may be so related at one or two removes. Thus a common form in

Baroque church interiors is the oval. This, like its spiritual forerunners of the megalithic era, may be based upon significant figures like the 3:4:5 Pythagorean triangle. Whilst the facades of Baroque churches and cathedrals still used combinations of root rectangles, the ground plans ran riot.

The buildings of Gianlorenzo Bernini admirably demonstrate the complexities of Baroque sacred geometry. His S. Andrea al Quirinale in Rome, built as a church for Jesuit novices between 1658 and 1670, was a transverse oval about seventy feet by forty, in deliberate defiance of the traditional orientation of the altar on the long axis. From this oval emerge eight side chapels, which, with the niche occupied by the high altar and the opposing entrance, gives a tenfold symmetry. Such a plan had never been attempted before, and has no spiritual parallel in geometric terms. Several years earlier, the eccentric sacred architect Francesco Borromini had constructed churches according to a modified ad triangulum system. Although a brief attempt to use ad triangulum had been made during the construction of Milan Cathedral, the system was exceedingly uncommon in Italy before the seventeenth century. Vitozzi's SS Trinita at Turin is perhaps the only example of an earlier date, and that was commenced as late as 1598.

Borromini's undoubtedly Baroque design for the Archiginnasio, later the seat of the University of Rome and later still of the Italian State Archives, incorporated the small church of St Ivo. This was designed on a plan of a Solomon's Seal, two interpenetrating equilateral triangles. The ground plan is embellished by developing the alternate vertices of the seal into simple semicircular bays and closing the others off halfway by convex features. Convex and concave walls thus interact with short straight interstitial walls to give an undulating interior which is nevertheless bound rigidly by its sacred geometry. Externally, St Ivo echoes the hexagon of the interior. A cupola surmounted by six buttresses rises to a central finial which is an anticlockwise spiral of three and a half turns, an echo of the ancient ziggurats of Babylon. Indeed, many contemporary illustrations of the Tower of Babel are of such a spiral form. The three and a half turns of the spiral finial are paralleled in the number of turns of the inner serpent Kundalini of Indian Tantric Buddhism. Borromini shows himself here as in receipt of arcane knowledge handled in a truly modern manner.

In the conservative atmosphere of Rome, Borromini s genuinely Baroque vision received little enthusiasm. Unlike fashionable architecture, his works were based more on pure geometrical form than upon Vitruvian Man. Bernini criticized him on the grounds that his architecture was extravagant, for while other architects used the human frame as a starting-point, Borromini based his buildings on fantasy. To use unusual geometry was considered heretical, as it might involve principles and concepts external to the Christian faith. After all, it was not long since Giordano Bruno had been burnt at the stake for heresy (1600). His Neoplatonic idea of the universe as a harmonious whole was more or less acceptable to the Renaissance Catholic, but the neo-Pagan ideas expressed in his geometry were not. He had explicitly used geometrical diagrams to express the attributes of God, microcosmic figures for an understanding of the macrocosm.

The influence of Borromini was not stifled, however. His natural successor was Guarino Guarini, who designed the singular S. Lorenzo and the Cappella della S. Sindone in Turin. These buildings follow Borromini in their unusual use of ornament and layout. San Lorenzo was designed on the octagram with a series of dome supports reminiscent of much earlier practice, like the Great Mosque at Cordova, Spain (875). This octagramic pattern, set within a square, served for the nave' of the church, while an oval formed the sanctuary. However, like the work of Borromini, this oval masked a Solomon's Seal in the centre of which stood the high altar.

Guarini's other masterpiece was the chapel he designed for the storage of what is perhaps the holiest and certainly the most contentious relic of Christendom - the Turin shroud. Fitted between the choir of the old cathedral and the Royal palace, this chapel was conceived as a cylindrical structure surmounted by a modified *ad triangulum* dome. This ad triangulum was not straightforward, for it contained another Baroque oddity, ninefold symmetry. As built, the body of the chapel has ninefold symmetry which reduces to threefold symmetry at arch level. This in turn composes the vaulting. In the centre of this is a twelve-pointed star. In all, the vaulting consists of thirty-six arches and seventy- two windows, which emphasize a twelvefold symbolism.

The word Baroque tends to conjure up in many people's minds a rampant array of seemingly random ornament hanging as if by magic from a backdrop of disconnected Classical motifs arranged in a theatrically spectacular manner. The churches of central Europe, reconstructed in the Baroque manner after the devastating Thirty Years' War, fit this image. Such churches as Sváty Mikulas in Prague or the pilgrimage church of Vierzehnheiligen in Germany are probably typical examples of the best of such churches. Both have rectilinear exteriors which conceal powerfully curving interiors. Within a framework of rectangles, a series of vesicas, circles and ovals are expertly articulated.

At Vierzehnheiligen, the architect Balthasar Neumann made the ground plan totally independent of the vaulting plan, and thus two separate but superimposed geometries were combined. The principles of sacred geometry which had guided the Renaissance architects were modified and remodified until the geometry of the building was masked by a plethora of tertiary and quaternary geometries. In England, however, the old traditions were maintained until a later date.

Baroque Geometry

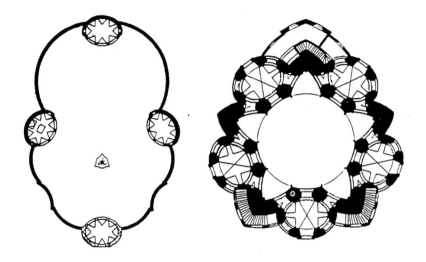

35. Giovanni Santin's baroque ground plans: left, the lower graveyard at Zd'ár, Czechoslovakia; right: the chapel of Svat`yJan Nepomuck`y, based on modified fivefold symmetry.

Sir Christopher Wren is probably the most famous English architect of all time. He alone among architects is mentioned in standard school histories, and his masterpieces in Oxford, Cambridge and London are admired annually by thousands of tourists who otherwise have no interest in architects. Wren was a scientist who came to architecture from a rationalist point of view. His spiritual mentor was naturally the ubiquitous Vitruvius, but Wren merely used his principles as starting points from which he simplified. When teaching at Oxford in 1657, he delivered a lecture in which he expounded his ethos:

> Mathematical Demonstrations being built upon the impregnable Foundations of Geometry and Arithmetick, are the only Truths, that can sink into the Mind of Man, void of all Uncertainty; and all other Discourses

Sacred Geometry

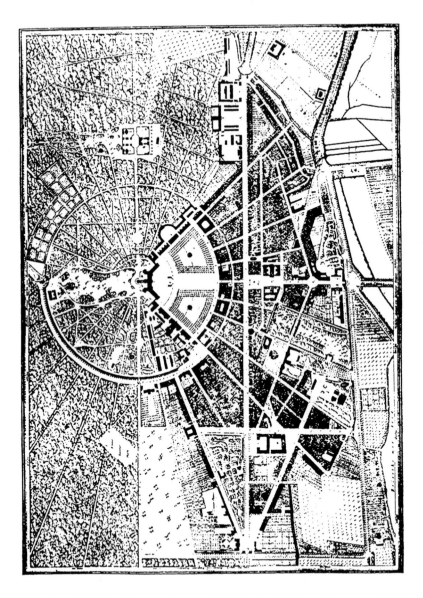

36. The layout of the Baroque town of Karlsruhe, Baden, Germany, laid out according to basic sacred geometry, the 32-fold division of the circle, in 1715.

participate more or less of Truth, according as their Subjects are more or less capable of Mathematical Demonstration.

Thus for Wren, geometry was the universal touchstone, the infallible and unchanging base against which all knowledge must be judged. His theoretical writings are few, as English architects tended not to indulge themselves in such practices, unlike their Italian counterparts. However, in Paretitalia, written by Wren s son, there is an appendix composed of four Tracts, ... rough Draughts, imperfect ...', which, although fragmentary notes, give an insight into the practice of sacred geometry in seventeenth-century England.

Tract I discusses the intentions of architecture, which 'aims at Eternity'. The discipline of architecture is ideally timeless and is therefore based upon the Classical Orders which are 'the only Thing incapable of Modes and Fashions', and as such represent the true canonical beauty, with an aesthetic basis grounded in geometry. According to Wren, there are two causes of beauty, the natural and the customary. Natural beauty derives directly from geometry, and geometrical figures are agreed as to a 'Law of Nature' to be inherently the most beautiful. Customary beauty is based upon association and is thus not grounded in transcendent principles, and consequently is inferior to that beauty derived geometrically.

In his City of London churches, and the masterpiece of St Paul's Cathedral, geometry can be seen as the guiding principle. This is especially apparent in the case of many City church steeples, which are little more than a pile of geometrical elements. This is not to disparage them in any way, as each element is masterfully blended with that immediately below it, creating Baroque structures at once elegant and exotic.

Even the dome of St Paul's can be geometrically reduced to a 'piling of the elements' comparable with a Tibetan Chorten, and having a similar symbolic interpretation.

Although the name of St Paul's Cathedral now evokes visions of a Baroque masterpiece, before the Great Fire of London in 1666 it was one of the greatest medieval cathedrals in Europe. Sited on the foundations of an even earlier church, this Gothic masterpiece possessed the tallest spire in England. At 555 feet, the spire remained the tallest structure ever erected in London until the construction of the Post Office Tower in 1965. The spire was lost in a fire in the sixteenth century, and the Gothic cathedral was irreversibly damaged in a disaster which incinerated much of the capital city.

Rebuilding of the cathedral had been mooted by 'Vitruvius Britannicus', Inigo Jones, the Court Architect, in the 1630s. His plans were never carried out. Even after the Great Fire, the remains were patched up for further use, but by 1672, when leaning walls and crumbling stonework threatened to bury the congregation in an avalanche of rubble, the cathedral was closed. Wren, who had earlier been appointed architect in charge of the fabric, grasped the opportunity to build a new cathedral.

After several plans and models, the final cathedral emerged. Based upon the Gothic *ad quadratum*, the design developed from an Albertian centralized structure to a traditional, plan, with nave, aisles, transepts and a long chancel. However, the major feature, a central space at the crossing, was retained. Geometrically, the parts of the cathedral were designed predominantly according to the ratio 3:2:1, although the ratio 2:1 is also common. Thus the nave is 41 feet wide and 82 feet high; the aisles 19 x 38 feet; the space beneath the dome is 108 feet wide and 216 feet high and the windows are 12 x 24 feet. The basic geometry of the ground plan of the whole building is drawn inside a double square 250 x 500 feet. This

Baroque Geometry

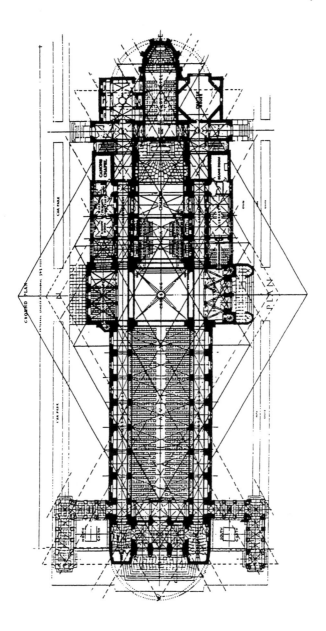

37. The ground plan of Guildford cathedral (1936-61), laid out according to *ad triangulum*.

Sacred Geometry

notional enclosure has the same proportions as the ancient fanes of the Step Pyramid, the Hebrew Tabernacle and the Temple of Solomon, points which would not have been missed by the operative freemasons under Thomas Strong whom Wren employed to build his magnum opus.

The overall height of the cathedral also adhered to mystic dimensions, being 365 feet from ground level to the top of the gilded cross mounted on the vast dome. This number, the number of days in the solar year, represents the consummation of God's year, the Cosmic Age when the Kingdom of Heaven is realized on Earth. This height of 365 feet was used in the 1930s in the Anglican cathedral at Guildford, where Sir Edward Maufe incorporated the measurement into his ad triangulum scheme. In addition to its annual connotations, 365 is equivalent in gematria to the name Abraxas, which, in addition to being the origin of the magic word Abracadabra, symbolises the consummation of all knowledge. Most importantly, the figure 365 feet is a geodetic measure, linked directly with the dimensions of the planet. It is one thousandth part of the length on the ground of one degree of latitude at London, which is 365000 feet. Wren, who once made a globe of the Moon for his patron King Charles II, would not have used such a measure casually.

13. Sacred Geometry in Exile

Although after the age of Wren and Newton there was a new secular world under construction, during the eighteenth century there was still an interest in the maxims of Palladio s musical harmony in building. In 1736 there appeared Robert Morris's book *Lectures on Architecture, consisting of rules founded upon Harmonick and Arithmetical Proportions in Building*. The ideas expounded in this late work followed the theory that, just as there are only seven degrees in music which can be discerned by the human ear, so only seven forms composed of cubes are appropriate to ensure elegance and beauty.

According to Morris, these were 1:1:1, the perfect cube; 1~i:1:1, the cube and a half; 2:1:1, two cubes placed end to end, 3:2:1, six perfect cubes; 5:4:3, sixty cubes, and 6:4:3, seventy-two cubes. The consistent harmonic proportions visible today in so many Georgian houses attest to their power over the minds of even speculative secular architects of the eighteenth century. However imperfect their interpretation of sacred geometry may have been, these architects still recognized that to create harmony one must begin with a geometrical framework upon which to prepare a design.

Sacred Geometry

By the nineteenth century, even much of the previous century's ideas had been debased into mere copyism. The only architects working with real forces were the civil engineers like Thomas Telford and Isambard Brunel, and later in the century Gustave Eiffel and Louis Sullivan, who produced buildings and structures whose proportions were necessitated by the constraints of engineering. Their contemporaries, meanwhile, in general contented themselves with carrying out slavish copies of Moorish, Gothic, Romanesque, Byzantine, Palladian, Chateauesque, neo-Renaissance, or, worse, outlandish mixtures and syntheses of these styles. The best of these stand to-day as wonderful idiosyncratic monuments, the spiritual forerunners of Disneyland. The worst have mostly long since succumbed to the demolisher's hammer.

Sacred architecture in the last century was mainly imitative. Vast piles like the Sacré Coeur in Paris, erected to commemorate the crushing of the anarchist Commune of 1871, embodied the geometry, but may, like the detail-perfect 'decorated' churches of Pugin, have had little mystic insight in their designs. Research on such matters is scanty. However, it can be said with some certainty that a large number of the churches which sprang up among the urban proletariat were merely designed as cost- effective exercises. Towns like Swindon and Crewe, dormitories for railway wage-slaves, were erected with the minimum of cost and planning, and so were their spiritual fanes.

On the other side of the coin, in the realm of the truly occult, the nineteenth century was something of a renaissance. Freed from the fear of inquisition, the power of the church having been broken by political revolution and scientific breakthroughs, the practitioners of the age-old occult sciences were able to come out into the open and put forward their theories and discoveries. A great interest in astrology, spiritualism and all kinds of magic arose. Necromancers like the French magus Eliphas Levi carried out evocations of the spirits of the dead - and published books of their results. In his magnificent work *Transcendental Magic, Its Doctrine and Ritual*, he describes in detail the evocation of the spirit of Apollonius of Tyana, the great Pagan miracle-worker of antiquity. In this act, the sign of the pentagram was carved upon a white marble altar brought especially for the purpose. After various rites, a being was indeed conjured up, but Levi's magic could not control such a powerful spirit, and he was soon lost.

Such a description of a magical operation could not have been openly published before the nineteenth century. Such was the loss of faith in Christianity's power that many 'fresh' ideas came into general circulation. Many of these concepts were derived from the ancient knowledge. In architecture, numerous ancient masonic and geomantic secrets were divulged in 1892 with the publication of W.R. Lethaby's Architecture, Mysticism and Myth. Five years later, William Stirling published anonymously his incomparable masterwork The Canon, which exposed the occult connections between the architecture of the ancients and magical and scriptural revelation. For the first time in history, many occult mysteries were published in easily comprehensible forms. The masonic secrets, which for many years had been leaked piecemeal into various books, were for the first time amalgamated with the diverse knowledge then being gleaned from the four corners of the world by anthropologists and folklorists.

Madam Blavatsky's books *The Secret Doctrine* and *Isis Unveiled* brought much oriental and Egyptian esoteric knowledge into a form readily available to the Western mind. Indeed the influence of her 'theosophical' thought has had a profound influence upon the twentieth century, ranging from the writings and architecture of Rudolf Steiner to the modern buildings of the De Stijl group and even, by way of the doctrine of the root races, to the racist theories of the German Nazis. The occult Order of the Golden Dawn and its many

Sacred Geometry

splinter groups also made available much of the arcane metaphysical knowledge of the ancient and medieval magicians. Combined with this great revival of occult knowledge, the massive strides in science and technology witnessed in the nineteenth and twentieth centuries have made it possible to investigate the underlying physical structure of matter and the organic geometry of the plant and animal kingdoms.

However, the reader will know only too well that this is a materialist age, so although these arcane principles were

38. The Versica Piscis in the window of the Wesleyan Methodist Church, Cambridge, built in 1913 - a continuation of ancient practice in the twentieth century.

published, their application in everyday life was still and is in a covert manner. The principles of sacred geometry, so well known by now, nevertheless still carry within them the age-old power, and their application still produce the desired effect. However, this belief is now unfortunately a minority interest. The majority of people remain unknowing, as indeed did their counterparts throughout history.

By the beginning of the twentieth century, the cult of enlightenment had made it impossible for an architect to admit that he was working according to esoteric principles. Just as geomancy had been largely extirpated, and everywhere on the surface of the Earth was considered equally profane, so sacred geometry was seen merely as a superstitious adherence to a system with no worth beyond tradition. In fact, things had gone even further. Most architects were not even conscious that there was a tradition.

A typical book of the period, *Hints on Building a Church*, by Henry Parr Maskell (1905), gives scarcely any guidance on canonical measures. His knowledge of sacred geometry was minimal, and yet he wrote an influential work on church-building. By 1905, only those architects who were versed in ancient masonic lore, or indeed practising freemasons, were interested in the niceties of canonical geometry. Much of the interest had passed to the academic architectural theorists like Lethaby.

Maskell wrote: 'Our forefathers trusted a good deal to what modern psychology calls the sub-conscious mind ... The "inner sense" was making all the calculations unconsciously. We must owe that this faith was justified, as a rule, in their works, even to the more abstruse matters of acoustics and ventilation.' This, of course, is nonsense. One does not erect by 'unconscious means a cathedral like Salisbury with a four hundred foot spire which has stood for seven hundred years. Such buildings are the result of an advanced technology of

Sacred Geometry

architecture, planned according to the sound principles of geometry. By the beginning of this century, the idea of progress, brought home so forcibly by recent technological advances like telecommunications, the electric light and powered vehicles, made it unthinkable that the builders of the Middle Ages should have possessed intelligent planning. The working drawings of medieval architects lay forgotten in cathedral libraries, so the 'unconscious' theory was a convenient excuse.

The psychological ideas of writers like Maskell must have been conditioned by the recent work of psychologists like C.G. Jung. In his earliest work, Jung discussed the fantasies experienced by an hysterical medium he had studied. In *On the Psychology and Pathology of So-Called Occult Phenomena*, he first put forward the concepts of 'archetypes' and the 'collective unconscious'. Jung discovered that certain geometrical and symbolic patterns tended to recur spontaneously in the drawings, paintings and dreams of his patients. The ancient concepts of the Gnostic philosophers and the Christian Qabalists, especially their symbolism, occur spontaneously throughout his works. He believed that these occult patterns were therefore spontaneous images in people's minds. Writers like the seventeenth-century mystic Jakob Boehme dwelt upon geometrical and alchemical symbols which, Jung claimed, were just as important in the modern age as signposts to the geography of the mind as they were in Boehme's century as symbols of the Divine Principle.

These ideas were turned back-to-front by writers like Maskell, who saw in the symbolism of the cathedrals the mindless operation of ignorant automata, carrying out their task in an unconscious manner. Jung had shown that the spontaneously generated archetypal patterns corresponded perfectly with the traditional symbolism of sacred geometry, so such an interpretation was inevitable. The orthodox mainstream of sacred geometry had by now been relegated to the books and magazines of occult bodies and to the theories of eccentric individuals like Claude Brighten and Antoni Gaudi.

Antoni Gaudí is an outstanding, if enigmatic, figure in modern architecture. A devout Roman Catholic, Gaudi saw every action as an act of piety, none more so than his architecture. For convenience rather than rationale, art historians categorise his unique works of canonical fantasy in the catch-all ragbag of art nouveau. Writers have tended to emphasize the bizarre or innovatory aspect of his outstanding work to the detriment of the canonical tradition in which he consciously operated. Yet underlying the organic incrustations, the polychrome tiles, broken ceramic dolls, tendrillous ironwork and nightmarish landscapes is a system of sacred geometry whose origins may be traced back to the medieval ad triangulum of Milan Cathedral and the proportional schemata of Vitruvius.

Unlike many other exponents of modern sacred geometry, Gaudí was totally orthodox in his religious beliefs. He was a Roman Catholic, with a special devotion to the cult of the Virgin. Each day of his long life, he attended the appropriate religious services, in later years walking several miles to do so. Naturally, his forte was church design, though he also designed several unique apartment blocks. One of these, the Casa Mila, was intended to act as the base for a vast effigy of the Virgin. This oddity, however, was never completed, for construction straddled the anarchist uprising of 1909 when many religious foundations were the butt of merciless attacks from the anticlerical insurrectionists. After the bloody suppression of the uprising, Gaudí's patron feared another, perhaps successful, revolution, and declined to brand his property in this manner. The anarchist commune which ran the city during 1936 did indeed attack churches but spared the Casa Mila, so his refusal was realistic.

Gaudí's masterpiece, upon which building work still continues to-day, was the Expiatory Temple of the Holy Family (the Sagrada Familia). This vast edifice, which will take another century to complete, was conceived as a symbol of the Christian rebirth of the city of Barcelona. Gaudí worked for many years upon the project, which was still fragmentary at the time of his death in 1926. His plans and models were largely destroyed during the Spanish Revolution in the 1930s, but his followers subsequently reconstructed them from published material. The Sagrada Familia was intended to be the logical progression of Gothic architecture 'rescued from the flamboyant', using modern techniques to avoid the necessity for structural devices such as flying buttresses. In fact Gaudí's interest in esoteric geometry made him one of the first architects in modern times to employ the parabolic arch, and because of this, his buildings contain what at first glance appears to be a preposterous concept - leaning pillars. These, however, are the result of looking at the construction of a building as a whole, mechanically and organically integrating all the parts in a manner which spiritually, if not functionally, echoes the 'all- embracing' nature of Gothic architecture.

Unlike the 'copyist' buildings, the Sagrada Familia is truly in the tradition of sacred geometry, because it used the system to determine its forms. These forms, for the period truly modern, owe little if anything to past styles, and yet, because of their underlying geometry, are fit for the purpose to which they are put. This, and not the external form, separates truly sacred architecture from the merely contrived or derivative.

At the same period as Gaudí's major works, the ideas of the Rosicrucian revival and the theosophical discoveries of Madame Blavatsky were being synthesized by the occult genius of Rudolf Steiner into yet another new system, Anthroposophy. Neither magic nor religion, Anthroposophy attempted to fill a new niche between the artistic and the mystic. Steiner, the founder and mentor of the faith, constructed a headquarters building which was a reproduction of the spirit of ancient temples in all but name. Incorporating a true sacred geometry, this temple, known as the Goetheanum, was the culmination of several years' research. In 1911 Steiner gave a lecture titled *The Temple is Man*, in which he discussed the principles which underlie the temples of antiquity. However, he differed from the usual historicism of his contemporaries for he spoke not only of ancient temples but also of those of the future. These, of which his Goetheanum was to be one (although then it was known as the Johannesbau), were to differ from those of ancient times in being emblematical of man who has received spirit in his soul.

In 1914, at Dornach in Switzerland, Steiner began the construction of his magnum opus, the projected Johannesbau. By now he had moved from Theosophy to the new Anthroposophy, and hence the symbols which he had intended to use were by now considered obsolete. Having obtained the direction of his new Anthroposophical art from the world theory of Goethe, he changed the name of the temple to Goetheanum. Steiner believed that the Goetheanum was a development of temple design which stood in direct continuity from antiquity to his time. His ideas were consciously in the tradition which I have traced in earlier chapters - the temple as symbolic of the body of man. For the Goetheanum, a whole coherent theory of the symbolic spiritual evolution of architecture was erected. From ancient times, Steiner claimed, up until the time of the Temple of Solomon, the human principle reigned. Various characteristics of his being were expressed in the temple. At the time of Christ, the arch and the dome symbolised the incarnation of the living and the excarnation of the dead, and the later Gothic cathedrals, laid out on the pattern of the cross, symbolised the grave of Christ.

In the later medieval period, Steiner believed that a new style of architecture arose, with the intention of embracing all mankind and leading them to a risen Christ. However, this edifice lived only in poetry, the perfect Castle of the Grail. It was towards this symbolic ideal that Steiner strove.

The Goetheanum as built was a twin-domed structure which merged the domes in an unprecedented manner. Like ancient Pagan temples it was oriented east-west with the entrance at the eastern end. An ingenious design, based on the 3:4:5 Pythagorean triangle, served as a basis for these two domes which symbolised not only the fusion of the male and female principles, but also the structure of the human brain. It is in this analogy that the geometry is especially ingenious. In the brain, the focal intersection of the two circles which compose the basic geometry of the temple, lies the pineal body. In occult terms, this organ is the seat of the soul, the ancient third eye of our archaic forebears. Steiner saw the pineal in terms of the Grail.

Steiner recounted that the rounded, art nouveau forms of the Goetheanum were necessitated by a change in the function of a temple. In antiquity, man had to incarnate, and come to Earth from out of the Cosmic Spheres, so the temple had to be built in a rectangular form in order that the divine ego could reside within. In the modern age, however, man had risen from the grave and manifested himself in his etheric form. Because of this, the rounded form was appropriate. Also, because it symbolised the organic rather than the earthly world, it was made of wood, a material which conforms with Goethe's theory of metamorphosis. Unfortunately, Steiner's insistence on wood made it an ideal target for the arsonists who burnt it at the end of 1922.

Like an ancient cathedral, the Goetheanum was crammed with esoteric symbolism. Stained glass windows with suitable mottoes expounded the symbolic function of the temple. At the entrance, the symbolic window Ich shaue den Bau (I behold the building) demonstrated that the elevation was intended to depict a man standing upright, yet another instance of the temple as man. Such esoteric planning as part of a consistent ethos is typical of Steiner, the mystic genius. How atypical it is of the modern spirit!

During the carnage of the Great War, artists on the sidelines in neutral countries like Switzerland and the Netherlands were driven by the atrocious spectacle to reject the art of an era which had spawned the mayhem of the Western Front. Disillusioned artists in Zurich set up the anarchistic movement called Dada, which rejected the whole concept of art and proceeded to deliberately outrage the conventional. In the Netherlands, which possessed a long tradition of 'puritan' art, the new movement in art and architecture known as De Stijl evolved. Based upon unadorned straight lines, De Stijl was seen as a rejection of the floriated tendrils of art nouveau, which the artists believed to be decadent, and the multifaceted fantasies of the Wendirigen or Amsterdam School of architecture whose amazing structures still dominate parts of Amsterdam sixty years later.

De Stijl was consciously based upon metaphysical principles and geometrical proportion. Some of its concepts are derived from the writings of the Dutch Jewish mystic philosopher Spinoza (1632-77). His belief was that separate objects and individual souls are not at all separate but are actually integral aspects of the Divine Being. He wrote that 'all determination is negation': that the definition of things is only possible by stating what they are not. This involves defining things by their boundaries, the points at which they cease to be themselves and become something not themselves. Likewise, in the many theoretical writings of De Stijl, the constant emphasis is upon relationships rather than things: the underlying geometry is more important than the physical being.

Sacred Geometry

The architect Theo van Doesburg and the painter Piet Mondriaan, the leading lights of De Stijl, constantly stressed that their aim was the recreation of the universal harmony. Like Spinoza they believed that all emotions were disruptive of this equilibrium. Hence they strove through the application of unadorned geometry to transcend the temporary exigencies of the world. Spinoza had claimed that spiritual health lies in the love of a thing immutable and eternal. Mondriaan wrote, 'That which is immutable is above all misery and happiness: it is balance. By the immutable within us we are identified with all existence; the mutable destroys our balance, limits us and separates us from all that is other than ourselves.'

This is an unusual sentiment for a modern artist, for we tend to visualise the modern painter as a self-centred individualist. However, Piet Mondriaan was involved with the mystic; a member of the Dutch Theosophical Society, he kept a photograph of Madam Blavatsky in his studio. Theosophical artists were attempting to create a new order based upon ancient wisdom, but in a totally modern style. Artists like the modern painter Wassily Kandinsky and the composers Scriabin and Stravinsky, all striking innovators, were also adherents of the Theosophical faith.

In addition to the mystic influences of Spinoza and Blavatsky, there was also the effect of the contemporary Dutch mystic Dr Schoenmaekers. In 1916, when the idea of De Stijl was being discussed, Schoenmackers lived in Laren, the same town as Mondriaan and Bart van der Leck. In 1915, Schoenmaekers's influential book *The New Image of the World* was published, and in the following year another book *The Principles of Plastic Mathematics*. His mystical approach to geometry greatly influenced the ideas of the new movement. Schoenmaekers wrote: 'We want to penetrate nature in such a way that the inner construction of reality is revealed to us.' Being based upon such mystic concepts, a seemingly materialist and totally modern style is in reality underlain by

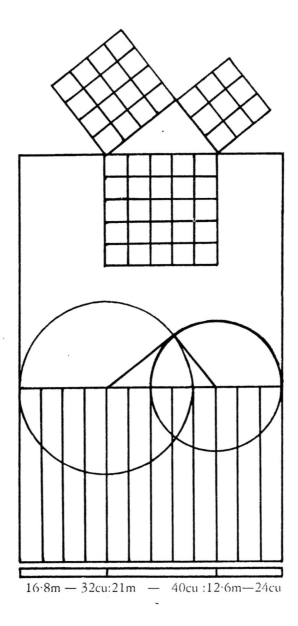

16·8m — 32cu:21m — 40cu :12·6m—24cu

39. The geometrical derivation of the two cupolas of the Goetheanum, based upon the 3,4.5 Pythagorean triangle, measured in Egyptian cubits.

an age-old ethos, merging it with the mainstream of occult thought which underlies architectural form.

The feeling in the 1920s that a new age was beginning was manifested in several diverse ways. In Germany, it led to the rise of Hitler and the new order of National Socialism. In Russia, the Bolsheviks attempted to restructure life in the image of Marxist philosophy. Artists rejected the old academicism and turned, like the De Stijl school, to what they considered as pure, essentialist, geometrical forms, devoid of ornament. Amid the proliferation of new creeds, the ancient Platonic sacred geometry surfaced once again. One of the greatest silversmiths of the twentieth century, Jean Puiforcat, created truly Classical works whose forms were based upon the ancient canonical systems of geometry and proportion. In a letter to Comte Fleury, written in 1933, Puiforcat explained how he discovered the system he used in his art deco cups and vessels:

> I plunged myself into mathematics and fell on Plato. The way was open. From him, I learnt the arithmetical, harmonic and geometrical means, the five famous Platonic bodies illustrated by Leonardo: the dodecahedron, the tetrahedron (fire), the octahedron (air), the icosahedron (water) and the cube (earth).

Puiforcat's designs, many of which still survive, bear such legends as 'Tracé harmonique, figure de départ $R\sqrt{2}$', and demonstrate that same striving for the timeless universal harmony that we find at all periods of artistic endeavour.

In the same vein of universality, the proportional system devised by the modern architect Le Corbusier appeared several years later. By 1950, in a period of relative optimism and a belief that world government was just round the corner, Le Corbusier thought it terrible that the metrology of the world was still split into two opposing camps. The English-speaking nations still adhered to the English Imperial system of measurement whilst the rest of the developed world had adopted, officially at least, the metric system. Le Corbusier realized that proportion was the fundamental concern of architects and builders, and that measure was just a tool to facilitate construction. Faced with a building practice which operated both in France and North America, he had come up against the nearly insuperable problems of working with two incommensurable systems of measurement.

In order to overcome this difficulty, and to set up a means of creating harmonious proportion, Le Corbusier went back to the ancient Greek canon of the Golden Section. From this, by means of many complex geometrical experiments, he came upon a coherent proportional modular system which he called *Modulor* - the module of the Golden Section. Like Puiforcat's, Le Corbusier's geometry derived from Plato and the Greek geometers, a geometry which would have been recognisable to Alberti or Wren. The Modulor was devised as a measuring tool. Like the ancient sacred geometry it was based jointly on abstract mathematics and the proportions inherent in the human frame.

A man with upraised arm provides the determining points of his occupation of space: the foot, solar plexus, head and the tips of the fingers of the upraised arm produce three intervals. These are points in a Fibonacci Series, a series of Golden Section ratios. From this 'natural measure' is derived a complex of subdivisions which forms the working core of the Modulor. But even with a system based solely on ratios, some starting measure is required.

Originally, Le Corbusier made his starting-point a hypothetical man 1.75 metres tall - a 'French height' as he later called it. The modules developed from this starting-point unfortunately proved unwieldy and incommensurate with everyday living. So Le Corbusier decided to find a better

Sacred Geometry

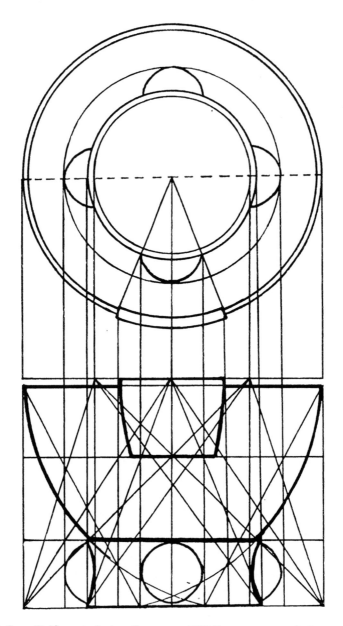

40. Jean Puiforcat: design for a cup (1934), root rectangle harmonic decomposition.

starting-point. His collaborator Py noted that in English detective novels the heroes, such as the policemen, are invariably six feet tall. Starting at this 'English height' of six feet, translated into metric at 182.88 centimetres, a new Modulor was drafted. To their delight and surprise, the divisions of this new Modulor, based on English measure, translated themselves into round figures of feet and inches - not surprising for a natural system of measure.

Le Corbusier continually asserted that his foot-derived Modulor was inherently based upon the human scale, as geometricians had proved, especially during the Renaissance, that the human body is proportioned according to the golden rule. This quasi-mystical approach is ever-present in the work of Le Corbusier. Although schooled and couched in the terms of early twentieth-century materialism, echoes of the earlier ethos of man as the microcosm shine through. His statement that architecture must be a thing of the body, a thing of substance as well as the spirit and of the brain, perfectly encapsulates that fusion of the physical, the spiritual and the intellectual which has been characteristic of the best architecture grounded in sacred geometry.

Le Corbusier repeatedly talked about 'loitering in front of the Door of Miracles', and to break through that door he went back to the Golden Section. Each and every object in his office was eventually placed according to the Modulor, a rigid and unyielding system, close to an unconscious form of geomancy. Yet although it was based upon sound ancient principles, the rigid use of the Modulor come-what-may is only using part of the available methods. With the technology of the modern world, it uses only the intellectual hemisphere of the brain, rejecting the intuitive. The geomancers and geometricians of old always tempered their geometrical patterns with pragmatic intuition, but the modernist tendency in all things is towards extremism, forcing one system on the world to the exclusion of all others.

Sacred Geometry

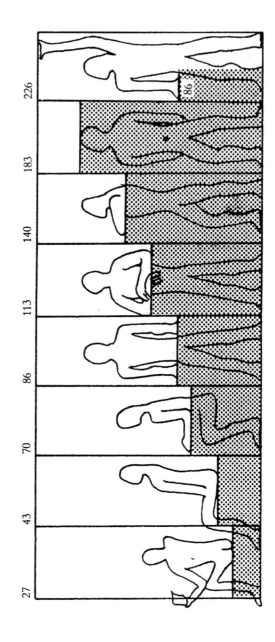

41. Le Corbusier's Modulor. The different positions of the human body during various activities fits the Modulor grades, bringing it into line with the ancient metrology of all nations.

14. Science: The Verifier of Sacred Geometry

The discovery and application of electricity by Faraday, Edison, Siemens and Tesla during the nineteenth century laid the foundations of the modern era. Cities could grow with cheap public transport provided by the electric tram, and electricity could power everything from underground trains to lighting and telecommunications. This new energy was found by its pioneers to be subject to various unthought-of laws. Occultists, fascinated by the new energy, began to see in its circuitry and physical expressions a parallel with their powers.

'Power' in the form a channelable energy analagous to electricity had been studied by magicians and novelists alike. Exemplified as the fictitious *vril* of Bulwer Lytton's novel *The Coming Race*, the existence of similar power had been reported from various parts of the globe by anthropologists. The mysterious maria of the South Seas which is said to have raised the vast stone statues of Easter Island was compared with the reported yogic energies of Asiatic holy men. Among influential writers, Madame Blavatsky and James Churchyard discussed the possibilities of these energies.

The scientific experiments of the physicist Chladni and others pointed the way to an understanding of the link-up between energy and geometrical patterns. Chladni discovered that a thin film of sand spread upon a mechanically-vibrating plate would form certain fixed geometrical patterns which were related to the wavelength of the vibration. Recent researchers on ancient mysteries have suggested that the possible wavelengths of telluric forces may determine the geometries of sacred buildings. This is likely, considering the age-old notions about the harmony of the spheres, the fundamental wavelength-geometry of the created universe. Patterns of power now being detected by dowsers in various parts of the world and by Paul Devereux and his Dragon Project team at the Rollright Stones may fit into this category. Those who have dowsed energy in ley lines believe that this energy may be part of a global grid which has a precise geometric form. Some people even link these patterns to the appearance of UFOs, ghosts, psychic disturbance and the occurrence of spontaneous combustion in humans.

The invention of the microscope in the seventeenth century and its perfection in the nineteenth led to the creation of a whole new scientific subject, the study of microscopic structures. With the discovery that animals, and plants in particular, are composed of regularly-structured cells, a renewed interest in geometry was born. Scientists attempted to create a theoretical basis for the geometrical structures which they were observing. Great scientists like Lord Kelvin put their minds to studying the geometrical packing of cells and came up with the age-old Archimedean and Platonic forms. Work by F.T. Lewis showed that the cellular structure of various vegetables tend greatly towards the Archimedean body of the 14-hedron (tetrakaidekahedron).

D'Arcy Thompson, who combined an encyclopedic knowledge of Classical writings with an extremely perceptive approach to biology, made perhaps the greatest contribution to our understanding of the divine harmony. In his seminal work On Growth and Form, published in the crucial year of 1917 (the year of the Russian revolution, Einstein's *Theory of Relativity* and the founding of De Stijl), Thompson traced the intimate relationships between the morphology of organic structures and the physical forces which mould the cosmos.

Thompson stated that basic structure is ultimately the same in both the living and the non-living, and can thus be determined by a physical analysis of the material system of mechanical forces. It represents an intrinsic harmony and perfection, something exhibited by a musical instrument in tune, the work of true craftsmen and all that is 'together' in nature. Orthodox science at present asserts that the structural forms of living organisms are totally controlled by an innate genetic pattern imprinted within the nucleus of each cell. Thompson believed that the shapes of various organs and organisms were moulded by the physical forces which act upon them. He found that the shape of these structures echo exactly the form of the physical force. The myriad forms of organic structure exist in conformity with the laws which govern all things. Their incredible beauty originates in the balance which is intrinsic in their 'natural' form, their conformity to the innate geometrical laws of the universe. The shell of the Pearly Nautilus is formed according to the equiangular spiral, as are the horns of certain sheep. Other classical geometrical forms occur throughout nature.

Thompson's organic metaphysics has never been well thought of by orthodox scientists. His evolutionary ideas were and are out of vogue, and his holistic approach runs counter to the reductionist tendencies of modern science. On the other side, his scientific approach has rendered his ideas apparently inaccessible to those interested in the esoteric side of life. Thus his work remains little read in those areas where it could reveal further insights. Thompson's ideas, while discounted by establishment science, cannot be refuted. Perhaps it is statements like the following which place him outside the pale of materialist science and inside the mainstream of Western occult thought:

> I know that in the study of material things, number, order and position are the threefold clue to exact knowledge; that these three, in the mathematicians' hands, furnished the 'first outlines for a sketch of the universe ... For the harmony of the world is made manifest in form and number, and the heart and the soul and all the poetry of Natural Philosophy are embedded in the concept of mathematical beauty.

Twenty years after Thompson's book appeared, electronics technicians in Nazi Germany perfected a tool which was to revolutionise our knowledge of the inner microscopic world of nature - the electron microscope. This new instrument, using electrons rather than visible light, enabled scientists to view structures thousands of times smaller than had hitherto been visible with light microscopes. It was not until the 1950s that techniques of specimen preparation enabled biologists to study the structure of living organisms with any measure of success. However, when many unicellular plants and animals were examined, they were found to bear unexpected structures (known as scales') whose arrangement and form adhered closely to the ancient schemata of sacred geometry. Being organic structures produced according to the laws enumerated by Thompson in *On Growth and Form*, they again demonstrate in a forcible manner the divine harmony. The marine organisms which the author has personally studied with the electron microscope demonstrate the principles of ad triangulum and ad quadratum developed by the masonic masters of the Gothic era. These are indeed reflections of the natural order of the universe.

The ancients' ideas of the universal order as an aspect of the creator are being verified by science. No longer can they be dismissed as the fantasies of ignorami. In the respected scientific journal Nature for 12 April 1979, an article by B.j. Carr and M.J. Rees appeared. Titled *The Anthropic Principle and the Structure of the Physical World*, it covered in a highly,

The Comacines and Medieval Sacred Geometry

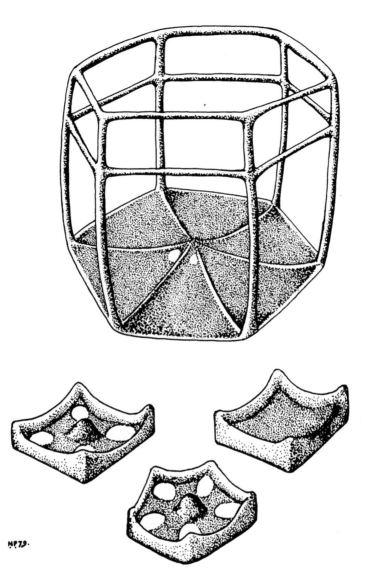

42. 'Scale' of Pyramimonas virginica. Upper sacle based on sixfold symmetry. Lower scales based on square and pentagon, size smaller than the wavelength of visible light.

technical and mathematical way the microphysical 'constants which govern the basic features of galaxies, stars, planets and the everyday world. The authors pinpointed 'several amusing relationships between the different scales' of the universe. For instance, the size of a planet is the geometric mean of the sizes of the universe and that of an atom, and the mass of man is the geometric mean between the mass of a planet and the mass of a proton. Other quite critical variables are delicately poised in the universal structure to enable life to exist. In the terms of materialist science these remarkable concurrences are just 'coincidence', but in metaphysical terms they are the fundamental necessity of the creator. The geometrical means represented by the planet and man echo the ancient worldview of microcosm and macrocosm. The only difference is the modern, non-metaphysical, terminology. It is not at all surprising to those of us who are aware of ancient teachings that modern cosmological research should verify the hermetic knowledge of the ancients.

The modern discoveries of science are naturally couched in materialist terms. However, all science is theory and as such is open to radical alterations in interpretation as and when new evidence is forthcoming from observation and experiment. The Everett many worlds interpretation of quantum mechanics postulated in 1957 states that at each observation the universe branches into a number of parallel universes, each corresponding to a possible outcome of an observation. Within such a framework, which was described by the anarchic playwright and author Alfred Jarry, in his neo-scientific novel *Exploits and Opinions of Doctor Faustroll, Pataphysician* and *Caesar Antichrist*, in which the observer becomes the most important character in the play of the universe, the anthropocentric figure in which the whole universal mechanism is comprehended - the figure of man the microcosm. In *Caesar Antichrist*, Jarry summed it up: 'I can see all possible worlds when I look at only one of them. God - or myself - created all possible worlds, they coexist, but men

The Comacines and Medieval Sacred Geometry

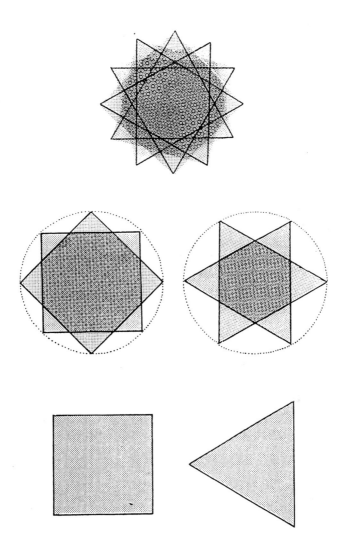

43. Ad quadratum and ad triangulum.

can glimpse hardly even one. This was written half a century before the Everett many worlds idea.

J.A. Wheeler in the book Gravitation, published in 1971, stated this poetic-philosophical concept in a scientific mathematical form. He envisaged an infinite ensemble of universes, each with varying physical constants and laws. Most of such universes would be stillborn, incapable by dint of their peculiar physics and geometry of allowing any interesting action to occur within them. Only those which started off with the right laws and physical constants can ever develop to the stage where they become aware of themselves. Thus our extant universe, one capable of sustaining the material level of existence, is by its very nature a special case, with appropriate physics and hence geometry for existence. This underlying geometry, recognized since the dawn of mankind as something special, is in fact an archetype of the unique nature of this phase of creation which enables the existence of the material world. Each time a geometrical form is produced, an expression of the universal oneness is made; it is at once unique in time and place and also timeless and transcendent, representing the particular and the universal.

As long as the world and mankind exist, the symbolism of geometry will be used in sacred and secular buildings. Some periods will see its use without understanding, while others will involve new theories and concepts. But whenever and wherever it is used, it will encapsulate the nature of creation and the metaphysical patterns which underlie it.

Index

Abiff, Hiram:72
Adelard of Bath: 97
Agrippa, Cornelius : 65, 131
Alvarez, Professor Luis : 56
Aristagoras: 50

Bede, the Venerable: 93
Bernini, Gianlorenzo : 148
Black, William Henry : 40-41, 44
Borromini, Francesco: 148
Borst, Professor Lyle : 46, 109

Charlemagne: 93-94, 100, 143
Charpentier: 108-109
Cox:, 98

da Pisa, Leonardo: 28
da Vinci, Leonardo: 16

Demetrius: 50
Demoteles: 50
Devereux, Paul: 42, 176
Dryden, John: 74
Duris of Samos: 50

Ely, Reginald : 7, 119
Euclid: 78, 81, 95, 97

Fergusson, James: 62
Fibonacci, Leonardo Bigollo: 28, 171

Gaudí, Antoni: 163-164
Giovanni, Frate: 105, 151

Hambridge, Jay: 25
Heaword, Rose: 110
Heinsch, Josef: 30, 43-45
Herod:73
Herodotus: 50, 55
Hurley, William: 115

Imhotep: 51-52
Isis: 6, 48, 59, 159

Johnstone, Colonel: 40

Lethaby, W. R.: 159, 161
Lévi, Eliphas: 158-159
Lockyer, Sir Norman: 39-43, 48, 110

Maccabeus, Judas: 72
MacLellan Mann, Ludovic: 31-33, 36-39, 42
Mendelsohn, Erich:83
Michael, John: 41, 45
Michelangelo: 84, 140
Monmouth, Geoffrey of: 18
Morris, Robert: 157

Pacioli, Luca: 27, 29
Palladio: 84, 136-139, 143, 157
Pappus the Alexandrine: 19
Paulsen: 55
Penrose, Francis Cranmer: 79
Petit, Reverend: 102
Plato: 21, 29, 75, 77-78, 80, 84, 90, 136, 139-140, 170-171
Pliny: 19, 50
Pollo, Marcus Vitruvius: 83
Protagoras: 1
Puiforcat, Jean:170-172
Pythagoras: 26, 47, 74-75, 136

Röriczer, Matthäus: 123, 125-127

Siculus, Diodorus:50
Solomon, King: 23-24, 67, 69-71, 73, 141, 143, 148-149, 156, 165
Spira, Fortunio: 136
Stecchini, Professor: 63, 80
Stirling, James: 54, 65, 67, 159
Stow, John: 101
Strabo: 50

Vitruvius:21, 83-88, 90, 122, 132, 137, 139, 144, 151, 154, 163

Wastell, John: 117, 119
Watkins, Alfred: 42, 44
Wood, Herman Gaylord : 41, 64, 107
Wood, John: 41
Wren, Christopher: 151, 153-154, 156-157, 171

A selection of other titles from Capall Bann:
Available through your local bookshop, or direct, post free in the UK, from Capall Bann at: Freshfields, Chieveley, Berks, RG16 8TF.

West Country Wicca - A Journal of the Old Religion By Rhiannon Ryall
This book is a valuable and enjoyable contribution to contemporary Wicca. It is a simple account of the Old Religion. The portrayal of Wicca in the olden days is at once charming and deeply religious, combining joy, simplicity and reverence. The wisdom emanating from country folk who live close to Nature shines forth from every page - a wisdom which can add depth and colour to our present day understanding of the Craft. Without placing more value on her way than ours, Rhiannon provides us with a direct path back to the Old Religion in the British Isles. *This is how it was*, she tells us. *This is the way I remember it*. Both the content of what she remembers and the form in which she tells us, are straightforward, homespun and thoroughly unaffected. ISBN 1 89830 702 4   £7.95

"West Country Wicca is a real gem - it is the best book on witchcraft I have ever seen! Thank you Rhiannon Ryall for sharing your path with us." - Marion Weinstein

The Call of the Horned Piper by Nigel Aldcroft Jackson
This book originated as a series of articles, later much expanded, covering the symbolism, archetypes and myths of the Traditional Craft (or Old Religion) in the British Isles and Europe. The first section of the book explores the inner symbology and mythopoetics of the old Witchcraft religion, whilst the second part gives a practical treatment of the sacred sabbatic cycle, the working tools, incantations, spells and pathworking. There are also sections on spirit lines, knots and thread lore and ancestral faery teachings. Extensively illustrated with the author's original artwork. This is a radical and fresh re-appraisal of authentic witch-lore which may provide a working alternative to current mainstream trends in Wicca. ISBN 1-898307-09-1   £8.95

Celtic Lore & Druidic Ritual By Rhiannon Ryall
Inevitably the Druidic Path crosses that of any genuine Gaelic Tradition of Wicca, so this book contains much druidic lore. Background material on the Druids is included, explaining much of their way of viewing the world & enabling the reader to understand more fully their attributions in general & their rituals in particular. The book is divided into five parts: 1: Casting circles, seasonal sigils, wands, woods for times of the year, Celtic runes, the Great Tides, making cones & vortices of power, polarities & how to change them, the seasonal Ogham keys & Ogham correspondences. 2: Old calendar festivals & associated evocations, the "Call of Nine", two versions of the 'Six Pointed Star Dance', Mistletoe Lore, New Moon working, the Fivefold Calendar. 3: Underlying fundamentals of magical work, magical squares, the Diamond Working Area. 4: Five initiations, including a shamanic one, some minor 'calls', some 'little magics'. 5: Background information on the Celtic path, the Arthurian myth & its underlying meaning & significance, the Three Worlds of the Celts, thoughts regarding the Hidden Path & final advice. ISBN 1 898307 225   £9.95

Auguries and Omens - The Magical Lore of Birds By Yvonne Aburrow
The folklore & mythology of birds is central to an understanding of the ancient world, yet it is a neglected topic. This book sets out to remedy this situation, examining in detail the interpretation of birds as auguries & omens, the mythology of birds (Roman, Greek, Celtic & Teutonic), the folklore & weather lore associated with them, their use in heraldry & falconry & their appearances in folk songs & poetry. The book examines these areas in a general way, then goes into specific details of individual birds from the albatross to the yellowhammer, including many indigenous British species, as well as more exotic & even mythical birds. ISBN 1 898307 11 3   £10.95

Angels & Goddesses - Celtic Paganism & Christianity
by Michael Howard

This book traces the history and development of Celtic Paganism and Celtic Christianity specifically in Wales, but also in relation to the rest of the British Isles including Ireland, during the period from the Iron Age, through to the present day. It also studies the transition between the old pagan religions & Christianity & how the early Church, especially in the Celtic counmtries, both struggled with & later absorbed the earlier forms of spirituality it encountered. The book also deals with the way in which the Roman Catholic version of Christianity arrived in south-east England & the end of the 6th century, when the Pope sent St. Augustine on his famous mission to convert the pagan Saxons, & how this affected the Celtic Church.. It discusses how the Roman Church suppressed Celtic Christianity & the effect this was to have on the history & theology of the Church during the later Middle Ages. The influence of Celtic Chhristianity on the Arthurian legends & the Grail romances is explored as well as surviving traditions of Celtic bardism in the medieval period. The conclusion on the book covers the interest in Celtic Christianity today & how, despite attempts to eradicate it from the pages of clerical history, its ideas & ideals have managed to survive & are now influencing New Age concepts & are relevent to the critical debate about the future of the modern chrurch. ISBN 1-898307-03-2 £9.95

The Pickingill Papers - The Origin of the Gardnerian Craft by W. E. Liddell
Compiled & Edited by Michael Howard

George Pickingill (1816 - 1909) was said to be the leader of the witches in Canewdon, Essex. In detailed correspondence with 'The Wiccan' & 'The Cauldron' magazines from 1974 - 1994, E. W. Liddell, under his pen name Lugh, claimed to be a member of the 'true persuasion', i.e. the Hereditary Craft. He further claimed that he had relatives in various parts of southern England who were coven leaders & that his own parent coven (in Essex) had been founded by George Pickingill's grandfather in the 18th century. This book discusses the origin of the Gardnerian Book of Shadows and Crowley's involvement in it. Other fascinating subjects covered include the relationship between the Hereditary Craft, Gardnerian Wicca & Pickingill's Nine Covens, the influence of Freemasonry on the medieval witch cult, sex magic, the use of quartz globes to boost power, ley lines & earth energy, prehistoric shamanism, the East Anglian lodges of cunning men & the difference between Celtic wise women & the Anglo Saxon cunning men. This book provides, for the first time, a chance for the complete Pickingill material to be read & examined together with background references & extensive explanatory notes. It also includes new material on the Craft Laws, the New Forest coven & Pickingill's influence on the Revived Craft. ISBN 1 898307 10 5   Price £9.95

The Sacred Ring - The Pagan Origins of British Folk Festivals & Customs
By Michael Howard

From Yuletide to Hallowe'en, the progress of the year is marked in folk tradition by customs & festivals, recording the changing seasons. Some events are nominally Christian because the early church adopted many of the practices & beliefs of the pagan religions to supplant them. All over Europe, including Britain, seasonal customs & folk rituals dating from the earliest times are still celebrated. Some festivals belong to a seasonal pattern of the agricultural cycle, others record the mystical journey of the Sun across the sky, both dating back to pagan religions. Each is a unique happening combining Pagan & Christian symbolism to create seasonal celebrations which can be experienced on many different levels of understanding & enjoyment.

The old festivals & folk customs which are still celebrated all over the British Isles each year represent a survival of the ancient concept of a seasonal cycle based on the sacredness of the land & the earth. The Sacred Ring of the year is a reminder of our ancient past & is still a potent symbol for the 20th century. It reminds us of humankind's integral link with Nature, even in our modern technological society, which is reflected in the ritual pattern of the changing seasons of the ecological cycle. ISBN 1 898307 28 8   £9.95

The Inner Space Work Book By Cat Summers & Julian Vayne

A detailed, practical book on psychic and personal development using the Tarot, pathworkings and meditations. The Inner Space Work Book provides a framework for developing your psychic and magickal abilities; exploring techniques as varied as shamanism, bodymind skills and ritual, through the medium of the tarot. There are two interwoven pathways through the text. One concentrates on the development of psychic sensitivity, divination and counselling, as well as discussing their ethics and practical application. The second pathway leads the student deeper into the realm of Inner Space, exploring the Self through meditation, pathworking, physical exercises and ritual. Together, the pathways form a 'user friendly' system for unlocking all your latent magickal talents giving a firm grounding in many aspects of the esoteric. ISBN 1 898307 13 X   £9.95

Pathworking 2nd Ed. By Pete Jennings & Pete Sawyer

A pathworking is a guided meditational exercise, used for many different aims, from raising consciousness to healing rituals. No particular beliefs or large sums of money are needed to benefit from it & it can be conducted within a group or solo at time intervals to suit you. Learn how to alter your conscious state, deal with stress, search for esoteric knowledge or simply have fun & relax. It starts with a clear explanation of the theory of pathworking and shows in simple & concise terms what it is about and how to achieve results, then goes on to more advanced paths & how to develop your own, it also contains over 30 detailed and explained pathworkings. Highly practical advice & information is given on how to establish and manage your own group. ISBN 1 898307 00 8 £7.95

In Search of Herne the Hunter   By Eric L. Fitch

The book commences with an introduction to Herne's story & his relationship with Windsor, the oak on which Herne hanged himself & its significance in history & mythology. The next section investigates antlers & their symbology in prehistoric religions, together with a study of the horned god Cernunnos, the Wild Hunt & its associations with Woden, Herne etc. & the Christian devil. There is a descriptive chapter on the tradition of dressing up as animals & the wearing & use of antlers in particular. Herne's suicide & its connection with Woden & prehistoric sacrifice is covered, together with the most complete collection of Herne's appearances, plus an investigation into the nature of his hauntings. Photographs, illustrations & diagrams enhance the authoritative & well researched text. The book also contains appendices covering the 19th century opera on the legend of Herne, Herne & his status in certain esoteric circles & Herne & Paganism/Wicca. ISBN 1 898307 237   Price £9.95

Living Tarot By Ann Walker

A simple guide to the Tarot, for both divination and discovery of the inner self requiring no previous knowledge. This book commences with background information on how the Tarot works and a brief history of the origins of these fascinating cards. To get the best out of the Tarot, it is necessary to have both an intuitive understanding of the cards and a working knowledge of the basic understanding of their meanings. Ann passes on her knowledge and thoughts gained in over 20 years practical experience using and teaching the Tarot. She concentrates on practical information put forward in an easy to read, no nonsense style.

The book includes a number of layouts for the Tarot, from simple layouts for the beginner to more complex spreads for the more experienced practitioner. Also included are details on astrological connections with the Tarot and the use of the cards as aids to meditation. The text is well illustrated, making the information easy to follow and apply.

ISBN number   1 898307 27 X   Price £7.95

The Mysteries of the Runes By Michael Howard

The book follows the historical development of the runes from earlier Neolithic & Bronze Age alphabets & symbols & their connection with other magical & mystical symbols including the swastika, sunwheel, equal-armed cross etc. Historical references to the runes & their use in divination by Germanic tribes & the Saxons together with the Viking use of the runes in Dark Age Engl& are also covered. The Norse god Odin is discussed, as the shaman-god of the runes together with his associated myths, legends & folklore, the Wild Hunt, the Valkyries & his connections with the Roman god Mercury, the Egyptian god Thoth, Jesus & the Odinic mysteries. The magical uses of the runes are described, their use in divination with examples of their everyday use. Fascinating information is included on the runes discovered during archaelogical excavations, rune masters & mistresses, the bog sacrifices of Sc&anavia & the training of the rune master, both ancient & modern. The symbolism & detailed descriptions of each of the eight runes of Freya's Aett, Haegl's Aett & Tyr's Aett are given with divinity, religious symbolism & spiritual meanings etc based on The Anglo Saxon Rune Poem. Details on how to make your own set of runes are included, how to cast the runes for divination with examples of readings &suggested layouts & the use of rune magic. The final section covers Bronze Age Sc&anavia & its religious belief systems; the gods & goddess of the Aesir & Vanir, their myths & legends & the seasonal cycle of festivals in the Northern Tradition. Also discussed are the Web of Wyrd & the Norns, Saxon/Norse paganism & traditional witchcraft. ISBN 1-898307-07-0 £9.95

The Enchanted Forest - The Magical Lore of Trees By Yvonne Aburrow

This is a truly unique book covering the mythology, folklore, medicinal & craft uses of trees. Associated rhymes & songs are also included together with the esoteric correspondences - polarity, planet, deity, rune & Ogham. There is a short history of tree lore, its purpose & applications. A further section gives information on tree spirits & their importance. The text is profusely illustrated with line drawings by the author & artist Gill Bent. This book will appeal to anyone who likes trees.
ISBN 1-898307-08-3   £10.95

The Witches of Oz By Matthew & Julia Philips

This is a well thought-out & highly practical guide to Wicca, the Old Religion. The authors run a modern Wiccan coven based on a blend of Gardnerian & Alex&rian ritual. The book starts by answering the question 'What is Wicca?' in simple, straightforward terms. A brief explanation of the history of modern Wicca is given, the authors then go on to describe the working tools used in Wicca, the festivals, special celebrations - H&fasting (marriage), Wiccaning & a Requiem, how to set up a circle, the philosophy & ethics of magic & how to work it. There are also sections on children in Wicca, incense, suitable recipes & spells. What makes this book different from many others written on the subject is the practical no-nonsense advice & the straightforward explanations of what is done & why. As readers may guess from the title, the authors live in Australia, though Julia originally came from England. Of course the rites & information given apply equally to the northern & southern hemispheres. ISBN 1 898307 180   £8.95

Crystal Clear - A Guide to Quartz Crystal By Jennifer Dent

This book answers the need for a basic and concise guide to quartz crystal - solving the many confusions and contradictions that exist about this fascinating topic, without being too esoteric or straying too far from the point. Crystals particularly clear quartz crystals, evoke a response, which can not be rationally explained; they inspire a sense of the sacred, of mystery, magic and light. This book explores why crystals are important, their place in history, cleansing, clearing, charging, energising/programming your crystals and techniques for using them for healing. Also included is a chapter on the formation & scientific aspects of quartz which is written in a humourous style to help offset the generally mind-numbing effects of talking physics with non-physicists. Jennifer has worked with crystals for many years, using them for healing & other purposes. ISBN 1 898307 30 X   £7.95

The Sacred Grove - The Mysteries of the Forest By Yvonne Aburrow

The veneration of trees was a predominant theme in the paganism of the Romans, Greeks, Celtic & Germanic peoples. Many of their rites took place in sacred groves & much of their symbolism involved the cosmic tree; its branches supported the heavens, its trunk was the centre of the earth & its roots penetrated the underworld. This book explains the various mysteries of the tree & how these can be incorporated into modern paganism. This gives a new perspective on the cycle of seasonal festivals. "The Sacred Grove" is the companion volume to "The Enchanted Forest - The Magical Lore of Trees, but can be read in its own right as an exploration of the mysteries of the tree. ISBN   1 898307 12 1   £10.95

The Magical Lore of Herbs by Marion Davies

There are plenty of herbals around, but none like this This marvellous book concentrates on the magical properties, folklore, history & craft of herbs together with their medicinal uses where applicable. Why & how herbs are used, their mythical associations & symbolism, all are detailed within these pages. The use of herbs has long been associated with paganism & the Old Religion, this book provides a wealth of information not only for modern day pagans, but for everyone interested in this fascinating topic. Marion Davies has an immense practical knowledge of herbs & their uses in treating humans & animals in addition to their more esoteric applications. This knowledge, coupled with her highly readable writing style makes this a must for anyone interested in herblore. The detailed researched text is well illustrated with line drawings. ISBN   1 898307 14 8   £10.95

Earth Magic - A Seasonal Guide By Margaret McArthur   Edited by Julia Day

An introduction to the real feeling of The Old Religion, concentrating on giving information on this nature based religion in a simple, straightforward manner. The book starts with a background & introduction section, then goes on to describe the seasons of the year & their associated festivals, Earth Magic & the elements used in it. Food has always been an important part of the major festivals, Margaret passes on traditional recipes together with their meanings & associations. Many books have been written about the Old Religion, but most concentrate on giving out set rituals & wordings. This book is different in that it concentrates on encouraging readers to get the 'feel' for the elements, plants & other parts of nature & to work with them rather than try to subdue them. An important book for the 90's helping many seekers find a simple, satisfying path of beliefs. ISBN   1 898307 016 £9.95

The Lore of the Sacred Horse - The Magical Lore of Horses By Marion Davies

Man's debt to the horse (and it's relatives) is immeasurable. For thousands of years before recorded history, man pushed forward his civilisations and conquests on the back of a horse and viewed his domains between a horse's ears. Man and horse are inextricably woven together into a relationship which is without equal in the rest of creation. Even Man's 'best friend', the dog, cannot claim the impact of the horse. This noble animal has been food and transport, the innocent participant in Man's wars, at one time his Deity and the honoured companion of his Deities. The symbol of majesty and power. From seed-time to harvest, the horse has been at the forefront of agricultural economy. Even so, Man's faithful servant has known the full extent of cruelty and ingratitude, may the Gods forgive us. The past fifty years have seen a dramatic increase in the popularity of the horse in our leisure pursuits and it once more takes it's rightful place - that of Man's companion.

This book traces this relationship from earliest times, stressing the religio-magical aspects. The Sacred Horse is rooted deep within our race-memory and is still to be found in our high-tech culture. ISBN 1 898307 19 9 £10.95